P9-ARU-834

Go to
CANADA
Your h. Commie
Pinko Red

GUIDE TO THE DRAFT

Selective Service rules and practices change frequently. Therefore, while this book—to the best of our knowledge—gives correct information to the date given below and while the general procedures and practices are unlikely to change greatly, specific rules may be changed at any time by administrative decision or court ruling.

It is important, therefore, that readers keep up to date by reading current newspaper and magazine reports.

This edition of *Guide to the Draft* was finally revised on

December 1, 1968

Guide to the Draft

by

ARLO TATUM

and

JOSEPH S. TUCHINSKY

Beacon Press   **Boston**

Copyright ©1969 by Arlo Tatum and Joseph S. Tuchinsky
Library of Congress catalog card number 69-17998

All rights reserved

Beacon Press books are published under the auspices of the Unitarian Universalist Association

Printed in the United States of America

ACKNOWLEDGMENTS

The authors are grateful to all those who have laid the groundwork for this book over the past twenty years. There are too many to list all by name, but we are especially thankful to those who have researched and written the memorandums, articles, and books used by draft counselors and attorneys, without whose efforts this book could not exist.

For reading sections of this book and making helpful comments, we are grateful to Dorian Allen, Kerry Berland, Peter Caplan, Eric Eldred, Alice Lynd, Harry F. Peck, Jr., George C. Pontikes, David Washburn, and Kale Williams.

For endless hours of devoted manuscript typing, we are thankful to Yuriko Hohri.

And to our wives, for understanding and forbearance which only the wives of draft counselors are called upon to give, our indebtedness can never be repaid.

Although the efforts of many people were indispensable to the compilation of this book, only the authors are responsible for any errors or shortcomings in it. We encourage readers to send to the authors or the publisher suggestions for improvements for future editions.

70140

Dedicated to those who struggle, against
all odds, to be human beings.

PREFACE

We have written *Guide to the Draft* because we believe that, as a draft-age man, you need to know your rights and obligations under the Selective Service System if you hope to have some control over your own destiny.

Many people have justly criticized the government for its failure to provide adequate information to draft registrants. It should be possible to go to a draft board and get a pamphlet fully explaining the regulations on deferments for men with dependents, on conscientious objection, on student deferments, or on physical standards, but no such publications are provided by Selective Service. Therefore, if you want to know your choices and rights, you must turn elsewhere. This book is our contribution to that need.

The draft is a controversial subject, related to hotly debated questions of military and foreign policy, and ultimately to the subject of what kind of society Americans want. Those who advocate positions on these subjects offer an important social and political service. But that is not the purpose of this book.

Our object is to explore the alternatives open to the man faced by decisions about the draft. We have tried to describe the choices, whether popular or unpopular, which might interest more than a few people. Since this is not a book for lawyers or expert counselors, we have tried to explain the details of each choice in nontechnical language.

Although we have strong opinions, we have tried to keep

them out of this book—despite the disappointment of friends who have urged us to point out the "rightness" of our, or their, positions.

All we advocate here is that you should get the fullest possible information, consider your choices carefully in terms of your own values, and make your own decisions. If you don't, your draft board will decide for you.

We believe that each man should try to control his own life, not allow a government agency or any other body to control him. Decisions about the draft involve questions of education, career, health, and marriage, of conscience and principle, of life and death. We believe each person to the extent possible should make such basic decisions for himself.

Making these decisions may not be easy. You may consult others—your parents, wife or girlfriend, a clergyman, teachers, or friends, and perhaps also a trained draft counselor or a lawyer—but ultimately, the decisions must be made in the loneliness of your own mind.

Our only hope is that your decisions will be right for you—and that you will still be glad you made them two or twenty years from now.

CONTENTS

LIST OF FORMS ILLUSTRATED

INTRODUCTION

The Alternatives

In the final analysis there are only five alternatives open to you after you are registered with a draft board:

1. Military service—by enlisting in active service or reserves, volunteering for induction, or being drafted (discussed in Part II).

2. Deferment or exemption until past draft age—by qualifying for one or more of the 12 classifications Selective Service offers. These may postpone induction until you reach 26, which is usually the age of safety from being drafted under present regulations (discussed in Part III).

3. Conscientious objection—by applying for and getting one of the two classifications which make you eligible to be drafted into noncombatant military service (usually in the Army Medical Corps) or into civilian alternate service, in place of combat service (discussed in Part IV).

4. Emigration—by leaving the United States for another country which will let you stay, with the likelihood that you will never be able to return (discussed in Part V).

5. Prison—for being convicted of refusing to obey Selective Service orders, because you aren't given the

classification you believe you should have or because you refuse to cooperate with the Selective Service System at all (discussed in Part IV).

The first alternative is only briefly discussed in this book because information about military service (including reserves) is available in many books and from recruiters. The other four alternatives are discussed in great detail here.

There are a few alternatives which don't fit easily into one of these five categories. A relative few men don't register and are never caught; most nonregistrants are eventually found and offered their choice between military service and prison. A few refuse orders and are never prosecuted. A few "go underground" by changing their identities and are never caught, but they must conceal their true identities for the rest of their lives, and for most this is neither possible nor attractive.

In addition, some men register while living outside the United States and are assigned to a special draft board for "foreign" registrants, which cannot induct them as long as they don't return to the U.S. before they are 26. Those who are rejected for physical, mental, or "administrative" reasons receive a type of deferment. Others bridge the gap of a few months or even years between the end of deferment and their 26th birthdays by using Selective Service procedures to stall for time; this may be considered a variety of deferment. The last three courses are fully discussed in this book.

Four abbreviations occur in square brackets [ ] throughout this book:

MSSA refers to the Military Selective Service Act of 1967, the law passed by Congress which is the basis of the present draft. Example: [MSSA 6(j)].

REG refers to the Selective Service Regulations, the rules issued by the President and the national director of Selective

Service under authority of the law. Example: [REG 1622.25].

LBM refers to the Local Board Memorandums issued by the director of Selective Service to advise draft boards on interpretations of the law and Regulations. Example: [LBM 17].

AR refers to Army Regulations, some of which affect Selective Service decisions. Example: [AR 40-501, 2-10b(5)]. The two-part number (40-501) identifies the regulation; the numbers and letters after the comma (2-10b(5)) identify the particular section within the regulation.

All of these may be consulted at any draft board, and the references are for those who want more detailed information than can be put into a handbook of this length or who need to point out these rules to their draft boards. All of these except some Army Regulations can be ordered from the Superintendent of Documents, Government Printing Office, Washington, D. C. 20402, by those who want their own copies.

They are also reprinted, along with important court decisions, in the *Selective Service Law Reporter* (abbreviated *SSLR* in citations of court decisions in this book), a subscription service for lawyers available at $18 to $42 per year from Selective Service Law Reporter, 1029 Vermont Avenue, NW, Washington, D.C. 20005.

On the following three pages is a list of all Selective Service classifications with a brief description of each and a short summary of your rights. Page numbers refer to the places in this book where fuller discussions may be found.

SELECTIVE SERVICE CLASSIFICATIONS

A draft board is required by law to place a registrant in the lowest classification for which it considers him eligible. The law requires a registrant to supply his draft board with full information concerning *all* classifications, and to notify it within 10 days of any change that might affect his classification. The classifications are listed in order below, starting with the highest [REG 1623.2].

Service Classifications	*See page*

I-A	Available for military duty.	75,95
I-A-O	Conscientious objector opposed to combatant duty and available for noncombatant duty only (usually Medical Corps).	207
I-O	Conscientious objector opposed to both combatant and noncombatant military duty and available for assignment to civilian alternate service.	209

Note: Conscientious objection (I-O or I-A-O), under the present law, is based upon (1) "religious training and belief," formal or personal, defined as a belief or value which is central to the individual's life, leading him to (2) opposition to "participation in war in any form," if (3) Selective Service believes he sincerely attempts to live in a manner consistent with his beliefs.   187

Deferment and Exemption Classifications

I-S	Deferment required by law for:		
	a)	Student who attends high school full time and is under 20 years of age: **I-S(H)**.	110

b) Student who has received an induction order while attending college full time; cancels induction order and defers until end of academic year: **I-S(C)**. Not renewable and may be received only once. | 126

I-Y Deferment for man qualified for service only in time of war or new declaration of national emergency, for physical, mental, or administrative reasons. | 165

II-A Deferred at discretion of draft board for employment (other than agriculture) which is "necessary to the maintenance of the national health, safety, or interest" or "essential community need." Given to most trades apprentices and to students in full-time trade, business, and vocational courses. | 129

II-C Deferred at discretion of draft board for essential agricultural employment; same criteria as II-A, plus consideration of farm's productivity and shortage of commodities produced. | 133

II-S Deferred for full-time college study:

a) Required by law for undergraduate if all the following conditions are met: (1) student has requested deferment by letter or Form 104, (2) school has sent Student Certificate (Form 109), (3) student is receiving credit for his courses toward a degree, (4) student is taking a full-time course load (as defined by his school), (5) student is making satisfactory progress toward finishing his degree in the usual number | 111 of years, and (6) student has not reached his 24th birthday.

b)   Required by law for students of medicine, dentistry, veterinary medicine, osteopathy, and optometry.   121

c)   At discretion of draft board for full-time graduate students in non-medical fields who entered their *second or subsequent* year of continuous study toward a doctoral or combined master's-doctoral degree in October, 1967— for up to a total of five years of continuous graduate study.   121

I-D   Deferment for man in reserves or senior R.O.T.C.   100

III-A   Deferred because of dependents:

a)   Required by Regulation if registrant notified local board of child (born or conceived) regularly living in his home; not available to those who have requested and received II-S student deferments since June 30, 1967.   138

b)   At discretion of draft board if evidence is provided that induction would cause "extreme hardship" to dependents; II-S student deferments since June 30, 1967, do *not* disqualify.   141

IV-B   Elected officials and judges of state or federal government deferred by law.   129

IV-C   Exemption for aliens not on immigration visas who have been in U.S. less than one year or have given up right to future U.S. citizenship, and alien registrants residing outside the U.S.   156

IV-D	Exemption for ministers of religion, divinity students, and full-time students pre-enrolled in seminaries.	154
IV-F	Deferment for man not qualified for any service for physical, mental, or administrative reasons.	165
IV-A	Exemption for man who has completed military duty, or is sole surviving son in family of which at least one member died as a result of military service.	162
V-A	Exemption for man over draft age (26 and over for those never deferred; 35 and over for those with "extended liability").	
I-W	Conscientious objector (I-O) performing civilian alternate service; **I-W(Rel.)**: conscientious objector who has completed alternate service but is not yet over age.	209
I-C	Member of the armed forces.	95

Notes

1. No classification is permanent; all may be reviewed and, if evidence warrants, changed upwards or downwards. 52

2. Upon receipt of any classification by a local board, you have a right to a *personal appearance with your local board* if you make written request within 30 days of the date on the classification card. On receipt of a classification resulting from a personal appearance, you have a right to *appeal to the state appeal board* if you make written request within 30 days of the date on that classification card. 57

3. For a personal appearance or appeal to be successful, it is important that you provide all available evidence in support of your request. | 14

4. All communications with the local board should be in writing, sent by *certified mail,* return receipt requested. These receipts and copies of all correspondence should be saved as important personal records. | 13,14

5. Under present regulations, men classified I-A and I-A-O who have passed pre-induction physical examinations may be inducted only in the following order: | 77

   a) Delinquents 19 and over (may be inducted even if they haven't previously received pre-induction examinations, but are examined at induction).

   b) Volunteers under 26, in order of volunteering (also may be inducted without previous examinations).

   c) Unmarried men and men married after August 26, 1965, aged 19 through 25, the *oldest* first.

   d) Men married by August 26, 1965, aged 19 through 25, the *oldest* first.

   e) Men aged 26 through 34 with "extended liability," the *youngest* first.

   f) Men aged 18 1/2 to 19, the *oldest* first.

Men in the last two categories have not been drafted since World War II. This call-up order is not necessarily permanent.

PART I

GENERAL PRINCIPLES

"If a registrant or any other person concerned fails to claim and exercise any right or privilege within the required time, he shall be deemed to have waived the right or privilege."

[REG 1641.2(b)]

CHAPTER ONE

THE NEED FOR DRAFT COUNSELING

No book can include enough information about the draft law and the actual practices of the nearly 4,100 draft boards to provide a complete guide for everyone. This book is intended as a concise, handy, and reliable guide for most registrants. It does not cover every problem that may arise.

Problems arise for a number of reasons. You may make mistakes and pass up your rights. Draft boards also may make mistakes and violate the Regulations. Little-known or confusing rules may cause you to go astray. Situations may arise in which you can choose among several alternatives, or claim several rights at the same time, and you may be unsure what to do and in what order.

Help is available. In most parts of the United States, especially in larger cities and on larger college campuses, there are experienced draft counselors.

WHAT A DRAFT COUNSELOR IS

Draft counselors can offer you help, usually free, if you want to know what your rights are, what choices are open to you, and how to deal with your draft board in the most effective way.

A good counselor will try to stimulate you to do your own thinking—to consider all the choices, not just the most obvious or popular ones, and to make decisions on the basis of your own long-range interests and the beliefs and values by

3

which you live. Naturally he has his own views, but he should not try to impose them on you.

Draft counselors have no connection with Selective Service. They are answerable only to the men they counsel and to their own ethical standards.

HOW TO FIND A DRAFT COUNSELOR

Independent draft counseling centers exist in a number of cities. Other draft counselors are associated with local or national organizations. In some areas, organizations like the American Friends Service Committee (Quakers), the War Resisters League, the Fellowship of Reconciliation, and Students for a Democratic Society provide draft counseling. So do some draft resistance groups.

Ministers, priests, and rabbis are increasingly getting training as draft counselors and offering aid to members of their religions and others. Some high schools, colleges, and universities recognize an obligation to provide students with reliable information and guidance, and see that teachers or counselors are trained as draft counselors. At many schools, student organizations provide draft counseling.

If you want to see a good draft counselor, you can usually find one by asking around your community or school. Chapter 21 of this book lists the addresses of some organizations which can refer you to a local counselor or provide information by mail or telephone.

HOW TO RECOGNIZE A GOOD DRAFT COUNSELOR

As in every other field, draft counseling has good and bad practitioners. You will have to make your own judgment of the quality of the counseling you get.

Before he offers advice, a good draft counselor will ask many questions, either with a written questionnaire like the one on pages 6-11 or in discussion. He needs to learn what the draft board has done, what you have done, and what classifications you may qualify for.

A good counselor finds out what you want to do, and why. He asks enough questions to be sure you know all the possibilities open to you. If he finds that you aren't fully informed, he explains all the choices and their probable effects. He asks questions about your beliefs and values. He doesn't tell you what you should do; he encourages you to make your own decision.

No draft counselor knows the answer to every question. The good counselor never guesses. If he doesn't know an answer, he will say so, and if the information is important he will look it up or ask another counselor, an attorney, or one of the national service organizations which train and advise draft counselors.

A good counselor encourages you to stay in touch with him. Good draft counseling is rarely a one-shot affair. It may take weeks, months, or years for your decisions to be made and acted upon. The good counselor will remain available and encourage you to come back to see him as new questions come up, or make sure another counselor will know about the situation and be available for return visits.

_____, _____
Last Name   First Name

DRAFT COUNSELEE RECORD FORM

The information requested below will be kept confidential. It is needed so that all aspects of your draft status can be considered and all of your legal rights protected. Please give complete and careful answers to all questions that apply to you.

Date _____

Name _____ Age _____ Date of birth _____

Home address _____ Phone _____

_____ Zipcode _____

Present address _____ Phone _____

_____ Zipcode _____

Local Board No. and address _____

Selective
Service No. _____ Present classification _____ Date issued _____ Date expires _____

Statement of problem: _____

_____

_____

Classifications: Did you complete the Classification Questionnaire (SSS Form 100, usually sent to you by the draft board shortly after you register)? _____ Date returned _____

Initial _____

List in order all classifications you have received:

Date   Class   Appealed?   Date   Class   Appealed?

_____

_____

Armed Forces Physical Examination: Have you had a physical or
have you received an Order to Report for a Physical Examination?_____
                    Date of Certificate of
Date   City and State   Acceptability (DD 62)_____   Accepted or Rejected_____

_____

Did you sign the Armed Forces Security Questionnaire (DD Form 98)?_____

Induction Order: Have you received an Order to Report for Induction?_____

Date issued   Induction date   City and State   Comments

_____

Have you been counseled before?_____ By whom and where?_____

7

DEFERMENTS AND EXEMPTIONS

Student
I-S, II-S, Are you now When do you Are you receiving
II-A, IV-D a full-time expect to credit toward a
student? _____ graduate? _____ degree or diploma? _____

Name and location of school _____

What kind of program? (circle one) When did you begin this program? _____

high school
trade, business or vocational Major field _____
junior college
undergraduate Have you requested a II-S deferment
graduate since July 1, 1967? _____
ministerial
other _____ Have you had a I-S(C) deferment? _____

Has your school submitted a Student Certificate (SSS Form 109) _____ Date _____

No. of hours or credits required for degree _____ Hours or credits completed _____

Normal number of years required for degree _____ Last full year completed _____

Occupational Do you work? _____ Type of work _____
II-A, II-C,
IV-D Hours per week _____ Are you a regular or ordained minister? _____

Is your employer willing to request a deferment for you? _____

8

Dependency
III-A   Are you married? _____ Date of marriage _____

   Living together? _____ Is she pregnant? _____

Do you have any children living in your home? _____

Is anyone dependent on you for financial or other help? _____

What evidence have you submitted to the draft board? _____

Sole Surviving Son Did any member of your family die   Relation
IV-A   as a result of military service? _____ to you _____

How many brothers do you have now living? _____

Aliens   Are you a U.S. citizen? _____ If not, what nationality? _____
IV-C

   Are you in the U.S. on an immigration visa? _____ Other visa? _____

Physical, Mental,   Do you have a physical or psychological condition
or Administrative   which might make you ineligible for service? _____
I-Y or IV-F
   Describe: _____

What evidence, if any, have you submitted to your local board? _____

Have you requested a medical interview? _____ Recommendation _____

Have you ever been convicted of a crime? _____ Sentence _____

Do you now have a court case pending? _____ Date of trial _____

9

CONSCIENTIOUS OBJECTION   Do you have religious or other reasons
I-A-O or I-O   for objecting to military service?
                            If so, briefly state the grounds of your objection:

_____

_____

_____

Church or religious affiliation, if any_____

Have you read the HANDBOOK FOR CONSCIENTIOUS OBJECTORS?_____

Do you think you meet the CO requirements regarding:

    religious training and belief_____

    objection to participation in war in any form_____

Which possibilities would you consider?

    non-combatant service (probably as a medic)_____

    alternative service as a civilian_____

        prison_____

        emigration_____

Have you ever been in ROTC, the reserve (Armed or National Guard) or any other form of military service? _____

Did you claim to be a conscientious objector by signing Series VIII on the Classification Questionnaire (SSS Form 100)? _____

Have you requested the Special Form for Conscientious Objector (SSS Form 150)? _____

Date issued _____ Date returned _____

Did you request I-A-O (non-combatant) or I-O (civilian alternative service)? _____

Have you received an Order to Report for Civilian Work? _____

What actions, if any, have been taken on your claim? (Personal appearance, treatment of witness, appeal, advice from government appeal agent, contact with State or National Director, etc. Include dates.) _____

_____

_____

_____

_____

_____

CHAPTER TWO

BASIC PRECAUTIONS AND RULES

If you have decided to allow yourself to be drafted as soon as possible, or to leave the United States to avoid the draft, or to disobey the draft law and risk prison, you will have little use for this chapter.

But if you want to qualify for any of the deferments or exemptions, hope to be recognized as a conscientious objector, or prefer to pick your own time to perform military service, you will be wise to follow the suggestions in this chapter. They are designed to insure that you don't lose your rights by accident.

1. *Plan ahead.* Deferments end, sometimes sooner than expected. Physical standards and the ages of call-up change, sometimes suddenly. Learn the choices and think about them. Think about what you will do before you're actually faced with the decision. Talk with a draft counselor if that seems desirable, and with trusted family members and friends.

2. *Observe deadlines.* Forms must be returned within 10 days (30 days for Form 150) after the date they were mailed or given to you. A personal appearance or an appeal must be requested in writing within 30 days after the date the last classification card was mailed to you (longer if you are abroad). The 10 or 30 days start the day *after* the board mailed the item to you. If your envelope is *postmarked* by the last day, you have acted within the deadline, regardless of when it is actually received by the board [LBM 72]. But

postmarks are sometimes hard to read, so don't rely on them unless you have to.

3. *See a counselor before you act.* Every draft counselor dreads the interview in which he learns that the registrant has already written to his draft board or taken some other action—and has done something which will harm rather than achieve his objective—but the time limits have already passed. The counselor wants to help, but there isn't very much he can do. The best time to talk with a counselor is within or before the time allowed to take action, but before action has been taken. If you're going to send a letter or form to the draft board, write a rough draft and take it with you when you see the counselor; he can tell you whether it will be the best thing to send. This applies equally to conversations with lawyers.

4. *Keep a complete file.* Never throw away anything you receive from Selective Service. Save letters, forms, old draft cards. Always make carbon copies of letters you send and photocopies of forms you fill out. Get copies of letters and forms sent by others on your behalf; the easiest way is for them to give the letter or form to you so you can make a copy, then send the original to the draft board. Keep at least one copy, and several if possible; some lawyers and counselors suggest having five or six. If you haven't kept copies in the past, you can go to your draft board at any time to examine your file and copy anything in it, or send someone else with your written permission. Your draft board will also have photocopies made for you if you pay the cost. Save all of these items in a safe place, together, where you can find them quickly when needed. When you see a draft counselor, take your entire Selective Service file with you.

5. *Put everything in writing.* Any request to the draft board for a personal appearance, appeal, postponement, or the like,

must be in writing. Immediately after a personal appearance, write as complete, detailed, and objective a summary of it as your memory allows, and promptly send it to the local board for your file. Do the same after any discussion, by telephone or in person, with the government appeal agent or the draft board clerk. If you appeal or protest, only the written information will reach the appeal board or higher official. If you ever end up in court, only the evidence in your file will be considered.

6. *Get proof that your letters and forms were received.* The best way is to mail them by certified mail, return receipt requested (any post office offers this service for a 40¢ fee, in addition to postage). Save the certified slip and the return receipt in your file, attached to your copy of the item you mailed. Another way is to take the letter or form to the draft board in person, and ask the clerk to give you a receipt for it or to sign and date your own copy to acknowledge receipt of the original.

7. *Send evidence.* Don't count on the draft board to investigate your claims, write to your references, or verify the information you submit. It can, but usually it doesn't. Collect the most convincing evidence you can get and send it to the board. Sections of this book on particular classifications suggest the sorts of evidence you need. Take a witness to your personal appearances.

8. *Use all your procedural rights.* You have a right to both a personal appearance with the local board and an appeal to the state appeal board *every* time the local board reclassifies you. You may sometimes have a right to a Presidential appeal after the state appeal. If in doubt about your rights, simply write, "I request a personal appearance and an appeal," and date and sign it, including your Selective Service number; send this to the local board before the 30 days are over. Use

appeal rights even if it seems useless; it may not be. Read Chapter 5 for full details about your appeal rights.

9. *See the government appeal agent.* He's usually a lawyer, he's likely to be sympathetic to the draft board's view, and he may or may not be well informed about Selective Service rules. But he may know how the draft board functions, what its attitudes and prejudices are, what kind of evidence it is impressed by. If you convince him your request is reasonable, he may help convince the board. If the board is doing something wrong, he may straighten it out. He is by no means a substitute for an independent draft counselor, but he can do some things a counselor can't (for details, see Chapter 3). Write a summary of the conversation with him immediately after your meeting and send it to the local board for your file. If he gives good advice, he may help you. If he is ignorant of the law, prejudiced against you, or misleading, your summary of the interview might help you convince a higher official to act favorably, or might even help you win in court if you end up there. Talk over his suggestions with an independent draft counselor before you act on them.

10. *Send address changes.* The Regulations require you to send changes of mailing address to your local board within 10 days. This is important because the Regulations don't require that draft board letters and forms actually reach you—only that they be mailed to your last known address. If they don't get to you promptly, you may lose important rights, or be declared delinquent for violating the Regulations and be inducted into the army immediately. If you are studying or working away from home, you may be wise to have your draft board send mail to your current address rather than rely on family members to forward it, unless you are moving frequently and fear the mail would be lost.

11. *Have your mail opened if you're away.* When you're traveling, vacationing, or for any other reason away from home for more than a week, be sure a family member, neighbor, or friend will check your mail for Selective Service items. If something arrives that must be taken care of before your return, be sure he can reach you by telephone or telegraph so you can act to protect your rights. If you will be completely unreachable while traveling, notify your local board by letter before you leave, telling when you will return or have a new address.

12. *Keep your draft board informed.* The Regulations require you to notify the local board of any change that could affect draft status, within 10 days after you learn of it. This includes marriage, your wife's pregnancy, adoption of a child, separation or divorce, support of any other dependents; entering or leaving school; beginning or leaving a job that might be deferrable; realization that your beliefs make you a conscientious objector; discovery of physical conditions that might affect draft eligibility. This will not only enable you to receive deferments you are entitled to, but may keep you from being drafted as a delinquent.

13. *Don't believe everything you hear.* There is a lot of misinformation around. The stories you hear in the neighborhood and at school are often inaccurate. And remember that board members, appeal agents, and other Selective Service officials receive no training at all. The same is true of local board clerks, who may misinform you unintentionally. If you read this book carefully, you will probably know more than most draft board members, and at least as much as most draft board clerks. Don't assume you know everything, but don't believe something is true just because somebody at a draft board said so. Check it with a draft counselor if you can.

CHAPTER THREE

THE SELECTIVE SERVICE SYSTEM

The Selective Service System is a separate federal agency, directly under the President. Unlike any other part of the government, it is run mainly by military officers and unpaid civilian volunteers, with the important exception of the local board clerks.

This chapter describes the structure of the system, the principal officials who operate it, and the powers they have.

THE LOCAL LEVEL

Local Boards

There were 4,088 draft boards in the United States and its territories at the end of 1967. Every county has at least one, except for some rural areas where one local board may serve up to five counties. In heavily populated areas, a local board may serve only a part of a city. In general, a local board is supposed to serve an area with a total population of no more than 100,000 people.

In practice, the number of draft-age men in a local board area varies considerably. Three local boards have more than 50,000 registrants each; 147 local boards have fewer than 1,000 registrants each (these are July 1, 1966, figures, as reported in the *Report of the National Advisory Commission on Selective Service).*

Each local board must have three or more members. Typically a board has 3 to 5 members, and under the 1967 law, women as well as men may serve. Members are nominated by the governor of the state, usually on the advice of the state director of Selective Service, and appointed by the President of the United States. They must be at least 30 years old, and may not serve after they reach 75 or have been on the board for 25 years. They serve without pay and may not be members of the armed forces or reserves. Anyone can find out who the local board members are because their names must be posted in the public part of the office [REG 1606.62(b)].

Local board members must live in the county served by the board, and if the board serves only part of a county, should "if at all practicable" live in the area served by the board. In practice, minority groups, particularly Negroes, are under-represented on draft boards. The director of Selective Service reported that as of August 1968 only 822 local board members, or 4.7% of the total of 17,653, were Negroes, compared with 278 at the end of 1966 and 623 at the end of 1967 (*Selective Service,* October 1968). According to the National Advisory Commission report, most board members are business, professional, and other white-collar workers, except in rural areas where many farmers serve on boards. About two-thirds of draft board members have served in the armed forces.

The members of the local board have sole authority to classify and induct registrants. Legal decisions can be made only at meetings attended by a majority of the members. Most boards meet once a month for a few hours; some meet more often.

Although a local board can ask you to come to a meeting, this is rarely done. The only time you are likely to meet your local board is when you request a personal appearance as part of the appeal process (discussed in Chapter 5).

Clerks

Since the average registrant accepts whatever classification he is given, he seldom or never meets the draft board members given, he seldom or never meets the draft board members themselves. If you do to the draft board office, you will meet not board members but the full-time, paid clerks.

The principal clerk is the executive secretary, who may be assisted by additional clerks. In larger cities, a single office may contain a number of local boards and have a very large clerical staff.

The clerks have no legal authority to make decisions for the board, but their influence is great. Because the board members meet infrequently, most of the decisions are in fact made by the clerks and merely approved at board meetings. As full-time staff members, the clerks may be the only local Selective Service officials who take the time to become familiar with the details of the Regulations, and their advice is usually accepted by the board.

They may also be the best source of information if you want to know the actual practices of your board so you can present a convincing case for the classification you want. But you should be aware that clerks are often too busy to give full information, and sometimes don't know the rules themselves, so you should check what they say with an independent draft counselor.

Government Appeal Agents

Another source of information and help is the government appeal agent or his associate. He is usually a lawyer, appointed by the President on the recommendation of the governor of the state. His name must be posted in the public area of the draft board office.

In practice, his principal role is as advisor. You are notified of your right to see the appeal agent each time the local board classifies you I-A, I-A-O, or I-O so you may get information about your appeal rights. On your request, the local board clerk must arrange a meeting for you with the appeal agent or a suitable substitute [LBM 82].

The appeal agent is not an independent counselor, however. He is required "to be equally diligent in protecting the interests of the Government and the rights of the registrant in all matters" [REG 1604.71(d)(5)]. On October 26, 1967, the director of Selective Service instructed appeal agents to report to the local board any information they receive about possible violations of the Selective Service Act or Regulations. Of 4,800 appeal agents in the country, only 7 wrote to General Hershey to protest that reporting information they receive while giving legal advice would violate the ethics of the legal profession (*Selective Service,* December 1967).

In his dual role as advisor to the registrant and legal advisor and informant to the draft board, the appeal agent cannot necessarily be trusted to represent your interests adequately. Nor, as an unpaid, part-time volunteer, does the appeal agent always know very much about Selective Service rules. But he may be useful anyway, and you are wise to consult him.

First, the appeal agent may be able to tell you what kind of evidence the board expects to see, whether it will allow witnesses at personal appearances, whether it is generous or tight with the classification you are hoping to get. Second, if the appeal agent is convinced that your request is reasonable, he may be willing to help convince the board. On the board's invitation, the appeal agent can attend any meeting [REG 1604.71(c)(2)]. Third, if the board has acted illegally, the agent may help to get it to correct the error. And if you want the board to reopen your classification so you may have another opportunity to meet with the local board and appeal to the state board, the appeal agent can recommend reopening [REG 1604.71(c)(3)].

He also has several other powers. He can appeal a classification to the state appeal board at any time before an induction order is issued, while you can appeal only during a 30-day period [REG 1626.2(b)]. If the state appeal board has ruled unfavorably, as long as no induction order has been issued, the appeal agent has the power to recommend to the state director that it be required to reconsider, or that a Presidential appeal be allowed even if the state appeal board vote was unanimous [REG 1626.61(b)].

Some local boards also have "advisors to registrants" who have no specific powers except to give information.

Medical Advisors

An unpaid local physician appointed by the President on the nomination of the state governor may serve as medical advisor to a local board. His principal role is to give "medical interviews" to registrants who claim to have physical conditions which may disqualify them for military service. On his advice, you may be classified I-Y or IV-F without the bother and expense of a complete armed forces physical examination (for details, see Chapter 13). Since the state director can authorize any medical advisor in the state to advise any local board [REG 1604.61], no local board should deny the right to a medical interview because it does not have a medical advisor available.

THE STATE LEVEL

State Appeal Boards

There are 96 state appeal boards, at least one in each state or territory, and, within each state, one in every federal court district. Many of the 96 are divided into two or more panels.

Each state appeal board or panel consists of five members nominated by the governor and appointed by the President. They must meet the same qualifications as members of local boards. They must live in the federal court district served by the appeal board. The members of the appeal board are supposed to be "representative of the activities of its area" and therefore "should include one member from labor, one member from industry, one physician, one lawyer, and, where applicable, one member from agriculture" [REG 1604.22].

No registrant can appear in person before the appeal board. When you appeal the local board classification, your complete Selective Service file is sent to the state appeal board. Without meeting you or performing any investigation of their own, the appeal board members review the file and classify you as they think suitable. Then they send the file, their decision, and their vote back to the local board. Except in the rare cases when the appeal board is required to reconsider its decision or when a Presidential appeal is possible, this is a final decision.

State Directors

There is a state director of Selective Service for each of the 50 states and also for Puerto Rico, the Canal Zone, Guam, the Virgin Islands, the District of Columbia, and New York City (the latter has jurisdiction in the city of New York; the director for New York State has no authority in New York City), for a total of 56 state directors. Each is a salaried employee appointed by the President on the recommendation of the governor of the state.

About five out of every six state directors are military officers or retired officers, as are many of the members of their state headquarters staffs who make most of the day-to-day decisions.

The state directors have very great power. Among other things, they can order a local board to reopen a classification, and can appeal a classification to the state appeal board or order the appeal board to reconsider its decision. They can appeal a classification to the Presidential appeal board regardless of the vote of the state appeal board, and can postpone or cancel an induction order. They can use any of these powers at any time, even after an induction order has been issued.

In addition, most state directors send memorandums to local boards interpreting the Regulations and advising them on deferment and other policies. These can be read and copied at local boards or state headquarters. And a local board generally asks the advice of its state director when it is unsure what to do about a difficult case. The advice is not binding on the local boards, but local boards usually follow it as though it were the law.

THE NATIONAL LEVEL

Presidential Appeal Board

The Selective Service Act provides for an appeal to the President of the United States as the final level of appeal. These appeals are in fact considered by a three-member board appointed by the President. Its formal name is National Selective Service Appeal Board, but it is usually called the Presidential appeal board. Its members, unlike the members of local and state boards, are paid for their time. One member is Negro.

Although many registrants are dissatisfied with the decisions of state appeal boards, very few are able to appeal them to the Presidential appeal board. See Chapter 5 for the conditions under which a Presidential appeal is possible.

Director of Selective Service

The head of the Selective Service System since 1941 has been Lt. Gen. Lewis B. Hershey, who became 75 years old on September 12, 1968. His powers include all of those held by the state directors, and others as well. He has authority, as does the President, to issue Selective Service Regulations, which have the same power as the law passed by Congress. He also issues several types of advisory memorandums—principal among them the Local Board Memorandums and the Operations Bulletins—to guide local and appeal boards and state headquarters in setting policies and interpreting the law and regulations. These have no legal status, but are generally followed as faithfully as the law itself.

The director is assisted by a large staff, mostly military officers, in Selective Service National Headquarters in Washington, D. C.

CHAPTER FOUR

REGISTRATION, CLASSIFICATION, REOPENING

In this chapter and the next one, we will describe the official procedures and at the same time offer suggestions for making use of them.

These procedures should be followed very carefully if you are trying to get the classification you believe you deserve. A mistake may cost you important rights.

You should also watch closely to be sure your draft board obeys the Regulations and gives you all the rights you are entitled to. A draft board will generally correct its mistakes when they are pointed out by a registrant, though sometimes the help of the appeal agent, state director, or national director, or even a Congressman, is needed. But only you, aided by your draft counselor (or lawyer), are likely to discover the procedural errors.

Many court cases have been won by registrants because draft boards didn't follow the right procedures, and many have been lost because registrants didn't follow them.

REGISTRATION

In the U.S.

The law requires men of draft age, including nearly all American citizens, and most noncitizens living in the United States and its territories, to register for the draft [MSSA 3]. By order of the President (Proclamation 2799, July 20, 1948), a man subject to registration must go to the nearest draft board within 5 days after his 18th birthday, although no one is drafted before he is 19.

The only citizens exempt from registration are those in the armed forces, including the reserves and military academies, in the Environmental Science Services Administration, and most of those in the Public Health Service. If they leave these services, they must register with Selective Service within 30 days [REG 1611.2(a), 1611.4].

A number of categories of aliens are exempt from draft registration. Those admitted as permanent residents must register just as citizens do. But those admitted as temporary residents may be exempt from registration if they are representatives and employees of foreign governments, workers admitted for seasonal labor, students, reporters for foreign newspapers, and members of the immediate families of any of these [REG 1611.2].

In addition, treaties make temporary residents from 15 countries exempt from registration: Argentina, Austria, Costa Rica, China, Estonia, Honduras, Ireland, Italy, Latvia, Liberia, Norway, Paraguay, Spain, Switzerland, Yugoslavia. All aliens living in the Canal Zone, whether permanent or temporary residents, are exempt from registration [LBM 16]; aliens in other U.S. territories must register unless they are exempted for one of the reasons listed here.

Noncitizens living in the U.S. who don't fall into one of these exempt categories must register with a draft board just as citizens must, within 5 days after they turn 18. If they arrive in the U.S. after they become 18, they must register within six months of their arrival [REG 1611.1, 1611.5]. (See Chapter 12 for special rules on the classification of aliens.)

Men who are in asylums, jails, or similar institutions at the age of registration are registered by the institution when they leave it [REG 1611.6, 1613.41]. Ironically, this includes those who are sent to prison for refusing to register for the draft.

Those who are required to register sometimes fail to do it at the required time. Draft boards usually overlook a short delay. It is usual for a board to classify in the normal way a man who registers voluntarily days, weeks, and sometimes many months after his eighteenth birthday, though those who are very late are sometimes threatened with immediate induction into the Army as draft delinquents.

When a man who hasn't registered is discovered by the Selective Service System (typically because of a police inquiry when he is arrested for something else, or because a neighbor notifies the draft board), he is often given the choice between arrest and immediately entering the armed forces.

At the time of registration, you are required to give only general information, such as personal identification, address, age. The permanent address you give is important because it will determine which local board you are assigned to. If you live at several addresses at different times of the year, you have a right to decide which you regard as your permanent address for draft board purposes [REG 1613.12(a)].

If you register at a draft board which doesn't have jurisdiction over your permanent address, it will transfer the records to the proper local board.

The local board which is assigned at the time of registration is permanent; you can never transfer to another after you are classified. (For the one exception, see "Registration Abroad," below.)

Shortly after registration, the local board mails you a Registration Certificate, one of the two draft cards you are required to keep.

Registration Abroad

If you are an American citizen living outside the United States and its territories when you turn 18, you are required to go to an American consulate or embassy as soon as possible. There you will be registered for the draft and assigned to a local board at your permanent address in the United States.

However, if you don't give any address in the United States, you are registered with District of Columbia Local Board No. 100 (Foreign). As long as you don't enter the United States, present Selective Service policy is not to order you for physical examination or induction [LBM 73]. If you return to the United States and settle in a community, your registration is transferred to the local board there and you are subject to the draft like any other registrant of that local board [LBM 62]. Of course, if you have remained abroad until you have passed your 26th birthday, and haven't received any deferments, you will be classified V-A and be ineligible for induction even if you are transferred to an ordinary local board. This loophole in the draft rules seems intended primarily for the children of American diplomats and career military men abroad. If large numbers of men tried to take advantage of this policy, it probably would be changed.

Another policy which affects only a tiny number of Selective Service registrants forbids sending any mail to, or ordering physical examination or induction of, a registrant while he is in Cuba [LBM 73].

CLASSIFICATION

Classification Questionnaire (Form 100)

Shortly after registration, the local board to which you are permanently assigned will send you a Classification Questionnaire (Form 100). The form is reproduced starting on page 30.

You have 10 days to complete and mail back the Form 100. Since it is important to fill it in correctly if you hope to receive the most favorable classification you are entitled to, you need this time. Sometimes the clerk will give it to you at the time you register and ask you to fill it out on the spot. This is improper, and you should explain that you need the 10 days you are entitled to, and will take the form home and return it when it is due. Normally, however, the form is mailed to you a few weeks or months after you register. If you have a good reason, the board can extend the 10-day limit for returning it [REG 1621.10(b)].

The Form 100 should be filled out very carefully. The answers to it will determine your classification and perhaps how soon you may be drafted, if at all. If you need more space for any answer, you should use the blank lines on page 6 of the form or attach your own extra pages. You should also get letters, forms, or other evidence from members of your family, your employer, your school, your minister, your doctor, or others as needed to prove answers which may make you eligible for certain classifications, and this evidence should be given to you to return with the Form 100 (or to send as soon afterwards as possible). As with all Selective Service papers, you should make copies (by xerox or similar photocopy method) of the completed form and all related papers, and keep them together safely where they can be found when needed later.

Series I of the Form 100 asks for information about identification and address. Since it is important that you get mail from the draft board promptly to protect your rights, you should give the address where you actually get your mail.

Series II asks about past or present military service. If you have served enough time in the armed forces of the United

Form approved.
Budget Bureau No. 33-R102.13.

SELECTIVE SERVICE SYSTEM

CLASSIFICATION QUESTIONNAIRE

(Local Board Stamp)

DATE QUESTIONNAIRE RECEIVED
AT LOCAL BOARD ....

Date of Mailing ....

COMPLETE AND RETURN BEFORE ....

2. Selective Service No.

1. Name of Registrant (First)   (Middle)   (Last)

3. Mailing address (Number and street, city, county and State, and Zip code)

(The above items, except the date received back at local board, are to be filled in at the local board before the questionnaire is mailed.)

INSTRUCTIONS

The law requires you to fill out and return this questionnaire on or before the date shown to the right above in order that your local board will have information to enable it to classify you. A notice of your classification will be mailed to you. When a question or statement in any series does not apply, enter "DOES NOT APPLY," or "NONE," otherwise complete all series.

The law also requires you to notify your local board in writing, within ten days after it occurs, of (1) every change in your address, physical condition and occupational, marital, family, dependency and military status, and (2) any other fact which might change your classification.

Fill out with typewriter or print in ink.

Member, Executive Secretary, or Clerk of local board

30

STATEMENTS OF THE REGISTRANT

Confidential as Prescribed in the Selective Service Regulations

Series I.—IDENTIFICATION

1. Name	2. Date of birth
(Last) (First) (Middle)	
3. Other names used (If none, enter "None")	4. Place of birth
5. (a) Color eyes | (b) Color hair | (c) Height | (d) Weight	6. Citizen or subject of (country)
7. If naturalized citizen, give date, place, court of jurisdiction and naturalization number	
8. Current mailing address	
(Number and street or R.F.D. route) (City, town, or village) (County) (State) (Zip code)	
9. Telephone No. (If none, enter "None")	10. Social Security No. (If none, enter "None")
11. Name and address of person other than a member of my household who will always know my address	
(Name) (Address)	

SSS Form 100   (Revised 6–25–68) Supplies of previous printings shall be used until exhausted.

(1)

31

Series II.—MILITARY RECORD

(Use Page 6, if necessary)

1. If you are now on or have been separated from active military service enter: (*a*) Armed Force ....

(*b*) Service number .... (*c*) Date of entry ....

(*d*) Date of separation .... (*e*) Character of service ....

(*f*) Type of transfer or discharge ....

2. If you are now a member of a Reserve component (including the National Guard) give: (*a*) Name and address of unit ....

(*b*) Service number .... (*c*) Date of enlistment or appointment ....

3. If you are now a member of a Reserve Officer Training Corps or any other officer procurement program, state the program, the Armed Force, date of entry, and any identifying number ....

....

(Enter on page 6 military service other than in Armed Forces of the United States.)

Series III.—MARITAL STATUS AND DEPENDENTS

(Use Page 6, if necessary)

1. (*a*) I (check one) : ☐ have never been married; ☐ am a widower; ☐ am divorced; ☐ am married.

(*b*) I (check one if applicable): ☐ DO ☐ DO NOT live with my wife; if not, her address is ....

....

(*c*) We were married at ...., on ....

                                                (Place)   (Date)

2. I have .... children under 18 years of age of whom .... live with me in my home.

      (Number)   (Number)

3. If you have no child, other than an unborn child, attach a statement from a physician showing the basis for his diagnosis of pregnancy and the expected date of birth.

4. The following other persons are wholly or partially dependent upon me for support:

Dependent	Relationship	Age	Approximate Income (Annual)	Amount Contributed by Me
Name	....	....	$	$
Address				
Name	....	....	$	$
Address				

32

Name				$	
Address					
Name				$	
Address				$	

Series IV.—REGISTRANT'S FAMILY
(Use Page 6, if necessary)

List below all the living members of your immediate family who are 14 years of age or over (except those shown in Series III) including your father, mother, brothers, sisters, father-in-law, and mother-in-law.

Relatives	Relationship	Age	Can This Relative Contribute to Support of Claimed Dependents [1]
Name			☐ Yes ☐ No
Address			
Name			☐ Yes ☐ No
Address			
Name			☐ Yes ☐ No
Address			
Name			☐ Yes ☐ No
Address			
Name			☐ Yes ☐ No
Address			
Name			☐ Yes ☐ No
Address			

[1] If your answer is "Yes," state extent of ability to contribute in detail on page 6.

(2)

33

Series V.—OCCUPATION

(Use Page 6, if necessary)

If Engaged in Agriculture, Also Fill in Series VI

1. I am now employed as a (Give full title, for example: bricklayer, farmer, teacher, auto mechanic, steelworker. If not employed, so state.) ....

2. I do the following kind of work (Give a brief statement of your duties. Be specific.) ....
....
....

3. My employer is ....
(Name of organization or proprietor, not foreman or supervisor. Enter "Self" if self-employed.)

....
(Address of place of employment—Street, or R.F.D. Route, City, and State)

....
(Nature of business, service rendered, or chief product)

4. (a) I have been employed by my present employer since ....
(Month and year)

(b) I am paid at the rate of $...................... ☐ Per Hour ☐ Day ☐ Week ☐ Month.
(c) I work an average of .... hours per week.

5. Other business or work in which I am now engaged is ....
(Nature of business, if none, enter "NONE")

6. Other occupational qualifications, including hobbies, I possess are ....
....
....

7. My work experience prior to that described in items 1 and 2, this series, is ....

8. I speak fluently the following foreign languages or dialects ....
9. I read and write well the following foreign languages or dialects ....

34

Series VI.—AGRICULTURAL OCCUPATION

(Use Page 6, if necessary)

1. I have been engaged continuously in farmwork since ....
   (Month and year)

2. I am (check appropriate box) : ☐ Sole owner-operator of a farm ☐ Joint owner-operator with another ☐ Hired manager ☐ Cash tenant or renter ☐ Standing rent tenant ☐ Sharecropper ☐ Share tenant ☐ Wage hand (hired man) ☐ Unpaid family worker.

3. I (check one) : ☐ AM ☐ AM NOT personally responsible for the operation of the farm where I work.

4. The principal crops and livestock of the farm I operate or work on are:

Names of Crops	Acres Devoted to Each	Kinds of Livestock	Number of Each Now on Farm

5. Principal products marketed during the last 2 years ....

6. Total value of products sold from this farm during the last crop year $..

7. The number of year-round workers on this farm is .... of whom .... are hired hands.
   (Number)   (Number)

8. Other farm experience ....

(3)

35

Series VII.—MINISTER OR STUDENT PREPARING FOR THE MINISTRY

(Use Page 6, if necessary)

1. I have been a minister of the .... since ....

   (Name of sect or denomination)   (Month) (Day) (Year)

   and (check one): ☐ HAVE ☐ HAVE NOT been formally ordained.

2. I was formally ordained at .... by ....

   on (date) ....

3. I am a student preparing for the ministry pursuing a full-time course of instruction at the ....

   ....
   (Name and address of theological or divinity school)

   .... under the direction of ....
                                              (Name of church or religious organization)

4. I am a student preparing for the ministry under the direction of ....

   ....
   (Name of church or religious organization)

   pursuing a full-time course of instruction at the ....
                                                   (Name and address of school)

   leading to my entrance into ....
                               (Name and address of theological or divinity school)

   in which I have been pre-enrolled.

Series VIII.—CONSCIENTIOUS OBJECTOR

(DO NOT SIGN THIS SERIES UNLESS YOU CLAIM TO BE A CONSCIENTIOUS OBJECTOR)

I claim to be a conscientious objector by reason of my religious training and belief and therefore request the local board to furnish me a Special Form for Conscientious Objector (SSS Form 150).

....
(Signature)

Series IX.—EDUCATION

(Use Page 6, if necessary)

GRADE OR YEAR COMPLETED (a) (Line through all grades or years successfully completed) (Exclude trade or business schools)	ELEMENTARY AND HIGH SCHOOL												COLLEGE				POST GRADUATE				
1.	NONE	1	2	3	4	5	6	7	8	9	10	11	12	1	2	3	4	1	2	3	4	5

(*b*) I graduated from high school in (month) .... (year) ....

2. (*a*) I am a full-time student in (check one): ☐ High school ☐ Trade school ☐ Business school ☐ College

.... majoring in .... and expect to (check one):

(Name and address of institution)

preparing for ....
(Occupation or profession)

☐ Finish course on ....   ☐ Complete degree requirements on ....
(Date)   (Date)

(*b*) I will be a full-time student next semester at ....
(Name and address of institution)

3. (*a*) I have completed .... years of college, majoring in .... and (check one): ☐ HAVE ☐ HAVE NOT

at ....
(Name and address of institution)

received a degree.

(*b*) I have received the degree(s) of ....

Series X.—STATEMENT OF ALIEN

1. I was admitted to the United States for (check one): ☐ PERMANENT RESIDENCE ☐ TEMPORARY RESI-

DENCE on ....
(Date of entry)

2. My Alien Registration Number is ....
If you have not been admitted to the United States for permanent residence, enter on page 6 a supplemental statement setting out the date you first entered the United States, with the dates of each subsequent departure and reentry when applicable. Attach copies of documentary evidence in your possession verifying your claimed alien status.

(4)

37

Series XI.—PHYSICAL CONDITION
(Use Page 6, if necessary)

1. If you were ever found not qualified for service in the Armed Forces state (a) when ....
(b) where ....

2. If you have any physical or mental condition which, in your opinion, will disqualify you for service in the Armed Forces, state the condition and attach a physician's statement.

3. If you have ever been an inmate or a patient in a mental or tuberculosis hospital or institution, give the name and address of each hospital or institution, and the period of hospitalization.

....

....

Series XII.—COURT RECORD
(Use Page 6, if necessary)

1. I (check one): ☐ HAVE ☐ HAVE NOT been convicted or adjudicated of a criminal offense or offenses, other than minor traffic violations. (If "HAVE" box is checked, complete this series.)

Offense (other than minor traffic violations)	Date of Conviction (Month, Day, Year)	Court (Name and Location)	Sentence

2. I (check one): ☐ AM ☐ AM NOT now being retained in the custody of a court of criminal jurisdiction, or other civil authority. Specify ....
(Awaiting trial, on probation, on parole, etc.)

Series XIII.—SOLE SURVIVING SON

I (check one): ☐ AM ☐ AM NOT the sole surviving son of a family of which the father or one or more sons or daughters were killed in action or died in line of duty while serving in the Armed Forces of the United States or subsequently died as a result of injuries received or disease incurred during such service.

38

REGISTRANT'S CERTIFICATE

INSTRUCTIONS.—You are required to make the registrant's certificate. If you cannot read, the questions and your answers shall be read to you by the person who assists you in completing this questionnaire. If you are unable to sign your name, you shall make your mark in the space provided for your signature in the presence of a person who shall sign as witness.

NOTICE.—Imprisonment for not more than 5 years or a fine of not more than $10,000, or both such fine and imprisonment, is provided by law as a penalty for knowingly making or being a party to the making of any false statement or certificate regarding or bearing upon a classification. (Military Selective Service Act of 1967.)

I CERTIFY that I am the registrant named and described in the foregoing statements in this questionnaire; that I have read (or have had read to me) the statements made by and about me, and that each and every such statement is true and complete to the best of my knowledge, information, and belief.

Registrant
sign here

....
(Date)   (Signature or mark of registrant)

....
(Date)   (Signature of witness to mark of registrant)

If anyone has assisted you in completing this questionnaire, such person shall sign the following statement: I have assisted the registrant herein named in completing this questionnaire because ....

....
(For example—registrant unable to read and write English, etc.)

....
(Signature of person who has assisted)

....
(Number and Street or R.F.D. Route)

Date ....

....
(City)   (State)   (Zip code)

(5)

39

Series XIV.—STATEMENT OF REGISTRANT

(Refer to Series Number)
(Use additional sheets if necessary)

40

_____

(Signature of Registrant)

_____

(Date)

(9)

(Registrant Will Make No Entries on This Page)

Dates	Minutes of Actions by Local Board and Appeal Board and on Appeal to the President (Continued from Page 8)	Vote	
		Yes	No

(7)

43

(Registrant Will Make No Entries on This Page)

Dates	Minutes of Actions by Local Board and Appeal Board and on Appeal to the President	Vote	
		Yes	No

U.S. GOVERNMENT PRINTING OFFICE

(8)

(Continue on Page 7)

States or an allied country, you may be exempt from the draft in classification IV-A (see Chapter 12 for details). If you are in a reserve unit, the National Guard, or advanced college R.O.T.C., you probably are eligible for a I-D classification (see Chapter 8 for details). Full information should be provided if you think you qualify for either of these.

Series III and IV ask about marriage and family relationships. You normally must be put in classification III-A if you provide evidence that you have children or that your wife is pregnant (see details in Chapter 11). If your family members or other dependents would suffer "extreme hardship" if you were drafted, you should also be classified III-A, but this type of deferment is hard to get and takes careful proof. If you think you may qualify for the "extreme hardship" deferment, you should answer Series III and IV only after reading Chapter 11 of this book, and if possible talking with a draft counselor.

Series V asks about work and occupational skills. The answers may be used to give a II-A occupational deferment, either immediately or later when the skills are used. Apprentices are usually able to get this deferment, and so are some industrial, technical, and professional workers (see Chapter 10 for details). Evidence, usually a letter from the employer requesting the deferment, is essential.

Series VI asks about farm work and is the basis for giving the II-C deferment (discussed in Chapter 10). If you believe your work on a farm is essential, you should answer the questions about products and cash value carefully and attach a letter from the farm owner or manager requesting the deferment. The county agricultural agent usually has information about qualifying for this deferment and may be the most helpful advisor.

Series VII should be filled out carefully if you are eligible for the IV-D exemption as a minister or while preparing for the ministry (details in Chapter 12). You must receive this exemption if you are a minister as your "regular and customary vocation," whether or not you are ordained. You are also classified IV-D while a full-time student in a seminary or in a preparatory program leading to a seminary in which you are pre-enrolled, provided your studies are sponsored by a church or religious organization.

Series VIII should be signed if your beliefs make you opposed to participating in war. Signing it will cause the board to send the Special Form for Conscientious Objector (Form 150), so you should be prepared to fill this out too. See Chapters 14 and 15 for a discussion of this subject; all conscientious objectors need the help of a draft counselor. If you are a conscientious objector and also are eligible for a deferment (as a college student, for example), you should sign Series VIII and file Form 150 as soon as possible to get your claim on record. Doing so should not have any effect on deferments; the board shouldn't consider the conscientious objector claim while you are eligible for any deferments.

Series IX asks about education and is the basis for giving I-S(H) and II-S deferments, and sometimes II-A. If you are under 20 and a student in high school, you should get a I-S(H) deferment without difficulty, but you may be asked for a letter from the high school saying you are a full-time student. If you are a student in college, you will receive the II-S deferment only if you request it in writing (separately from this form) and have the school send its form to the draft board. The date you expect to graduate (question 3(a)) may be important; it might be difficult to get further deferments if you need more time than you estimated to complete school, so the *latest* probable date should be entered. If you are a student in a trade, vocational, or business school and are not working for a college degree, you should get a II-A deferment and need to have the school send a form or letter to the draft board. If you are entering college or other school next semester, you should specify where (question 3(b)) and attach a copy of your admission letter, receipt for a tuition deposit, or other evidence. See Chapters 9 and 10 for details of these deferments.

Series X must be completed if you are not a U.S. citizen but are required to register for the draft. The calculation of time spent in the U.S. is important because the IV-C classification is given only during the first one year in this country, whether in a single visit or several visits added together. See Chapter 12 for details.

Series XI asks about physical and mental conditions which might disqualify you from military service. Classifications I-Y and IV-F (discussed in Chapter 13) may be based on your answer to this question and the doctors' letters and other evidence which you should send with the form or as soon as possible afterwards. In most cases, however, the information isn't used until a medical interview or examination is ordered by the draft board. Although Selective Service files are supposed to be confidential, this isn't always true, and information about physical and mental conditions sent to Selective Service may get into the hands of other government agencies.

Series XII asks about criminal convictions and court custody. If you have been convicted of a felony (a crime that can be punished by more than a year in prison), you may sometimes, but not always, be classified IV-F. If you have a long record of minor convictions, you may possibly be classified I-Y or IV-F. If you are awaiting trial or are out on probation or parole, you cannot be drafted until you are out of the custody of the court. Copies of records to prove this status should be attached to the form if possible. See Chapter 13 for details.

Series XIII asks about eligibility for the IV-A exemption

(discussed in Chapter 12) as the only living son in a family of which at least one member died as a result of service in the U.S. armed forces. Evidence should be attached; the Veterans Administration may be the best source of evidence and advice.

You must sign and date the Form 100 on page 5. If someone else has written the answers, he must sign at the bottom of this page, but a lawyer or draft counselor who merely advises or gives information should not sign here.

The completed Form 100 becomes the basis for future draft classifications. The last two pages (the back cover and inside back cover) contain spaces where the draft board members or clerks will record all actions taken, including letters and forms sent and received, classifications and the votes by which they were given, and appeals. Since you have the right to examine and copy your file at any time [REG 1606.32, 1670.8], this is the first place you would go to learn what has been done and when. (Unfortunately, clerks record some actions by form numbers, so you may need to copy the list and take it to a draft counselor to figure out what the numbers mean.)

Initial Classification

Soon after the return of the Form 100, often at the next monthly meeting, the local board should classify you in the lowest classification it believes you are qualified for (considering I-A highest, and continuing in the order of the list on page xvi).

The board must consider all the information in the file, including any letters or forms you have sent with the Form 100 or later.

If you have indicated that you might be eligible for a lower classification than I-A, but haven't given enough information for the board to be sure whether you qualify, the board can

The law requires you to have this Notice in addition to your Registration Certificate, in your personal possession at all times and to surrender it upon entering active duty in the Armed Forces.

The law requires you to notify your local board in writing within 10 days after it occurs, (1) of every change in your address, physical condition and occupational (including student), marital, family, dependency and military status, and (2) of any other fact which might change your classification.

Any person who alters, forges, knowingly destroys, knowingly mutilates or in any manner changes this certificate or who, for the purpose of false identification or representation, has in his possession a certificate of another, or who delivers his certificate to another to be used for such purpose, may be fined not to exceed $10,000 or imprisoned for not more than 5 years, or both.

(LOCAL BOARD STAMP)

SEE OTHER SIDE

(Fold along this line)

SELECTIVE SERVICE SYSTEM
NOTICE OF CLASSIFICATION

This is to certify that

_____
(First name) (Middle initial) (Last name)

Selective Service No. _____

is classified in Class _____

until _____
by Local Board unless otherwise checked below:
☐ by Appeal Board
vote of _____ to _____
☐ by President

_____
(Date of mailing)

_____
(Member, Executive Secretary, or clerk of local board)

_____
(Registrant's signature)

SSS Form 110 (Rev. 5-25-67)
(Previous printings are obsolete)
(Approval not required)

DETACH ALONG THIS LINE

SELECTIVE SERVICE SYSTEM

This is your Notice of Classification, advising you of the determination of your selective service local board that you have been classified in accordance with Selective Service Regulations. The various classifications are described on the reverse side of this communication. You are required to have a Notice of Classification in your personal possession.

When a subsequent Notice of Classification is received you should destroy the one previously received, retaining only the latest.

FOR INFORMATION AND ADVICE
GO TO ANY LOCAL BOARD

(Sign here)

NOTICE OF RIGHT TO PERSONAL APPEARANCE AND APPEAL

If this classification is by a local board, you may, within 30 days after the mailing of this notice, file a written request for a personal appearance before the local board (unless this classification has been determined upon such personal appearance). Following such personal appearance you may file a written notice of appeal from the local board's classification within the next 30 days (or in the next 30 days after the date of mailing of notice of the new classification which results from such personal appearance but may result in no change of classification. If you do not wish a personal appearance but do want to appeal your case, you may do so by making such an appeal in writing, to your local board, within the specified time.

Appeal from classification by local board may be taken by filing written notice of appeal with your local board within one of the following periods after the date of mailing of this notice:

(1) 30 days (where the registrant is located in the United States, its territories, possessions, Canada, Cuba, or Mexico OR;

(2) 60 days (where the registrant is located in a foreign country other than Canada, Cuba, or Mexico).

You may file with your local board a written request that the appeal be submitted to the appeal board having jurisdiction over the area in which your principal place of employment or current place of residence is located.

If an appeal has been taken, and one or more members of the appeal board dissented from the local board's classification, or a written notice of appeal to the President with your local board within 30 DAYS after the mailing of this notice.

Your Government Appeal Agent, attached to your selective service local board, is available to advise you regarding your rights and liabilities under the selective service law.

Your Selective Service Number, shown on the reverse side, should appear on all communications with your local board. Sign this form immediately upon receipt.

FOR INFORMATION AND ADVICE, GO TO ANY LOCAL BOARD

GPO : 1967 O - 284 -141

SELECTIVE SERVICE CLASSIFICATIONS

CLASS I

Class I-A: Registrant available for military service.

Class I-A-O: Conscientious objector registrant available for noncombatant military service only.

Class I-C: Member of the Armed Forces of the United States, the Environmental Science Services Administration, or the Public Health Service.

Class I-D: Qualified member of reserve component, or student taking military training, including ROTC and accepted aviation cadets applicant.

Class I-O: Conscientious objector available for civilian work contributing to the maintenance of the national health, safety, or interest.

Class I-S: Student deferred by law until graduation from high school or attainment of age of 20, or until end of his academic year at a college or university.

Class I-W: Conscientious objector performing civilian work contributing to the maintenance of the national health, safety, or interest, or who has completed such work.

Class I-Y: Registrant qualified for military service only in time of war or national emergency.

CLASS II

Class II-A: Occupational deferment (other than agricultural and student).

Class II-C: Agricultural deferment.

Class II-S: Student deferment.

CLASS III

Class III-A: Extreme hardship deferment, or registrant with a child or children.

CLASS IV

Class IV-A: Registrant with sufficient prior active service or who is a sole surviving son.

Class IV-B: Official deferred by law.

Class IV-C: Alien not currently liable for military service.

Class IV-D: Minister of religion or divinity student.

Class IV-F: Registrant not qualified for any military service.

CLASS V

Class V-A: Registrant over the age of liability for military service.

SPECIAL NOTICE

A registrant who was deferred on or before his 26th birthday should ascertain from his local board if his liability has been extended to his 28th or 35th birthday. (See other side.)

ask you or others (employer, school, etc.) for more information. The board can also ask governmental and welfare organizations for information about you. And the board can ask you to come to a board meeting so it can ask you for more information before classifying you. But these things are not usually done. Most boards don't go out of their way to get information, leaving it up to you to send it if you want a lower classification.

When you have been put into a classification, the local board sends you a Notice of Classification (Form 110), usually called a classification card, the second card (along with the Registration Certificate) which you are required to keep. It shows the classification and the date on which it was mailed (an important date for appeal purposes), and sometimes the "expiration" date of the classification, the date on which the board plans to reconsider your classification. The Notice of Classification is illustrated on pages 50-51.

REOPENING

The first classification you get isn't necessarily permanent, even if you don't appeal or if you use up all your appeal rights and are still left in that classification. The local board may sometimes "reopen" the classification—that is, start the classification process all over again, consider all the evidence in the file, and place you in the lowest classification it considers you eligible for.

When a deferment expires, the local board reopens your classification and either renews your deferment or puts you in a different classification. If you send in new information, as you are required to do within 10 days after any change in your circumstances, the local board should look it over. If your evidence is for a *higher* classification, the board shouldn't reopen your classification as long as you qualify for the lower classification. For example if you send in a claim as a I-O conscientious objector while you are a college student classified II-S, or if you send in evidence for a II-A occupational deferment while you are a father classified III-A, the evidence would just be put into your file. But if you send information about a *lower* classification than your present one, the board should reopen your classification at its next meeting and consider giving you the lower classification.

The Regulations say a local board "may" reopen the classification on request "if such request is accompanied by written information presenting facts not considered when the registrant was classified, which, if true, would justify a change in the registrant's classification" [REG 1625.2]. Although the Regulations say the board "may" reopen when new facts are presented, many courts have ruled that it *must* reopen, provided the new facts are presented before an induction order is issued.

This book is intended for draft-age men, not lawyers, but so many draft boards seem not to know about these court decisions that a few important ones are listed here. The following court decisions hold that a board must reopen a classification when new facts are presented which, if true, would justify a change of classification, provided they are presented before an induction order is issued: *U.S. v. Freeman*, 388 F.2d 246, 1 SSLR 3012 (7th Circuit, 1967); *Miller v. U.S.*, 388 F.2d 973, 1 SSLR 3014 (9th Circuit, 1967); *U.S. v. Ransom*, 223 F.2d 15 (7th Circuit, 1955); *Townsend v. Zimmerman*, 237 F.2d 376 (6th Circuit, 1956).

You may make a request for reopening at any time. It may also be made by anyone who claims to be your dependent, or by an employer who is requesting an occupational deferment for you, or by the government appeal agent who serves the

POSTAGE AND FEES PAID
SELECTIVE SERVICE SYSTEM

SELECTIVE SERVICE SYSTEM
OFFICIAL BUSINESS

TO:

(LOCAL BOARD STAMP)

SELECTIVE SERVICE SYSTEM
CLASSIFICATION ADVICE

_____
(Date of mailing)

YOU ARE ADVISED THAT

_____ _____ _____
(First name)   (Middle initial) (Last name)

Selective Service No. _____

has been classified

in Class _____ until _____, 19____

by Local Board unless otherwise checked below

By { ☐ Appeal Board by vote of _____ to _____
    ☐ President

Date of mailing Notice of
Classification to registrant _____

Classification appealed from _____

_____
(Member, Executive Secretary, or Clerk of Local Board)

SSS Form 111 (Rev. 5-25-67) (Approval not required)
(Previous printings are obsolete.)

54

NOTICE OF RIGHT TO APPEAL

The registrant's Selective Service Number shown on the reverse side of this card, should be included in all communications with the local board.

Any person who claims to be a dependent of a registrant or any person who, prior to the classification appealed from, filed a written request for the current occupational deferment of a registrant, may appeal to the appeal board from classification by the local board by filing a written notice of appeal with the local board within one of the following periods after the date of mailing the Notice of Classification to the registrant, whichever is applicable:

(1) 30 days if the registrant is located in the United States, its territories, possessions, Canada, Cuba, or Mexico OR :

(2) 60 days if the registrant is located in a foreign country other than Canada, Cuba, or Mexico.

The person taking the appeal may file with the local board a written request that the appeal be submitted to the appeal board having jurisdiction over the area in which the principal place of employment or current place of residence of the registrant is located.

Any person who claims to be a dependent of a registrant or any person who, prior to the classification appealed from, filed a written request for the current occupational deferment of the registrant, may appeal to the President from classification by the appeal board by filing a written notice of appeal with the local board within 30 DAYS after the date of mailing the Notice of Classification to the registrant when one or more of the members of the appeal board dissented from such classification. There is no right of appeal from the decision of the President.

The local board of jurisdiction may permit any person who is entitled to appeal to the appeal board or to the President to do so even though the period within which the appeal may be taken has elapsed, if it is satisfied that the failure of such person to appeal within such period was due to a lack of understanding of the right to appeal, or to some other cause beyond the control of such person.

Each person who has filed a request for the registrant's deferment shall, within 10 days after it occurs, report to the local board in writing any fact that might result in the registrant being placed in a different classification, such as, but not limited to, any change in his occupational, marital, military, or dependency status, or in his physical condition.

★ U.S. GOVERNMENT PRINTING OFFICE : 1967 OF—265-366

55

local board. When requesting a reopening (or reclassification), it is sometimes helpful to ask for a meeting with the board to discuss your reasons.

When the local board reopens your classification, it mails a new Notice of Classification to you—and a Classification Advice (Form 111) to a dependent or employer who requested a deferment for you—showing your classification. Sometimes the classification will be the same as before, but the reopening is still desirable, for it gives you a new chance to get a personal appearance and appeal.

The Regulations do not allow reopening a classification after an induction order has been issued, "unless the local board first specifically finds there has been a change in the registrant's status resulting from circumstances over which the registrant had no control" [REG 1625.2(b)]. Therefore, it is important to submit all evidence and make all claims before an induction order is issued. Relatively few claims may be recognized after issuance of an induction order—for example, a hardship deferment if your father has suddenly died and you must support the family. If you are seeking reopening after issuance of an induction order, it may be especially useful to ask for a meeting with your local board (often called a "courtesy hearing").

(For pregnancy discovered after issuance of an induction order, see page 140; for conscientious objection claimed after issuance of an induction order, see page 193; for college students who receive induction orders during the school year, see page 126.

If a reopening is allowed, the induction order is automatically cancelled, except in a few unusual cases [REG 1625.14].

CHAPTER FIVE

PERSONAL APPEARANCE AND APPEAL

Every time you are classified by the local board, whether it is your first classification or not, you have at least two rights: a personal appearance with your local board and an appeal to the state appeal board.

This is true even if the new classification card has the same classification as the old one. And it is true every time the local board changes the classification, as when a deferment runs out and the board issues a I-A.

There are three exceptions. (1) If the new classification card is issued as a result of a personal appearance, you have only the right to appeal to the state appeal board; you can't ordinarily get another personal appearance immediately. (2) If the classification is a state appeal board decision, the box on the card marked "by Appeal Board" is checked and the vote is shown. In that case you can't have a personal appearance or a state appeal, but you can sometimes get reconsideration by the state appeal board or a Presidential appeal. (3) While there is no further appeal possible after a Presidential appeal, other steps may be possible.

There is no need to choose between a personal appearance and an appeal. You have a right to both, and except in unusual circumstances it is a good idea to use both.

This is true even if you have no convincing grounds for a lower classification. You have the right to these procedures, and at the least you may gain three to six months or more during which no induction order can be issued. By the end of that time your circumstances may have changed. If so, you may be eligible for a different classification and should send in the new information and request a reopening (discussed on page 52).

PERSONAL APPEARANCE

Request

If you want to meet with your local board, to try to convince it to give you the classification you want, you must request a personal appearance in writing within 30 days after the date your classification card was mailed to you.

Your request does not have to be in any particular form. A letter saying, "I request a personal appearance," would do. You should include your Selective Service number, the date, and your signature. Of course it is better if you also explain in this letter why you think your classification should be changed, and include evidence you want the board to consider. Sometimes the board will give the desired classification without a personal appearance, on the basis of the letter and evidence, but the personal appearance should be requested anyway so the right won't be lost.

All Selective Service deadlines should be taken seriously, but the 30 days allowed to request a personal appearance should be considered especially important because the Regulations discourage the board from granting late requests [REG 1624.1(a)]. Despite this, some boards *have* granted late requests when good reasons were given, so there is no harm in trying if the deadline has already passed. The 30-day period begins on the day *after* the board mails the classification card. If your letter is postmarked on or before the 30th day, your request must be granted, even though the letter was received after the 30 days ended [LBM 72].

The personal appearance can't ordinarily be transferred.

This may mean inconvenience and travel expense if you live far from the local board, but the effort may impress the board with your sincerity. If you are having difficulty getting the classification you want by corresponding with the board, you should usually consider it worth the trouble and cost to present your arguments in person, and to answer their questions. The personal appearance is the *only* chance you ever have to meet the Selective Service officials who are making the decisions about you. Where the classification you want is a matter of judgment rather than an automatic right, the personal appearance is the most important part of the process, far more likely to succeed than the state appeal.

If it is impossible to travel immediately to a personal appearance, the board will sometimes agree to a reasonable delay—until a school vacation, for example, if a student can't return home until then.

If there is no time when you can travel to a personal appearance, as a last resort you can ask your local board to allow you to appear before a board where you are then living. This courtesy is sometimes allowed in place of a personal appearance. The nearby board meets with you and sends your local board a report. Your local board then makes its decision without meeting personally with you.

If even this isn't allowed, you will have little choice but to pass up your right to a personal appearance and just appeal to the state appeal board.

If you aren't sure you will get to the personal appearance, but want to keep the possibility open while making sure you will have the right to appeal to the state appeal board, you may want to request both rights in the same letter. This letter might begin, "I request a personal appearance. If the personal appearance doesn't result in the classification I am applying for, I also want to appeal to the state appeal board."

Preparation

There are several things you can do to prepare for a personal appearance. First, you may want to talk with a draft counselor. Second, you may want to talk with the government appeal agent or the local board clerk, or both of them, to ask what sort of evidence the board requires, why the board didn't give the desired classification, how much time you should expect to have, whether the board usually admits witnesses, and what its attitudes are toward the classification you requested. (The clerk should arrange an appointment with the appeal agent on request.) Third, you should go over the evidence you have submitted to be sure nothing helpful, or essential, has been forgotten; the draft counselor may help with this. Fourth, you should prepare a very simple outline, perhaps on an index card, of the things you want to say at the meeting; you should take this with you as a reminder, look at it occasionally during the meeting, and be sure you mention everything you intend to.

If you are applying for one of the harder classifications to get (I-A-O, I-O, II-A, II-C, III-A because of extreme hardship, and sometimes IV-D), you will probably want to take a witness to the personal appearance. The Regulations allow a local board to admit witnesses but don't require it to [REG 1624.1(b)], so you and your witness should be prepared for the possibility of refusal. But even if you know in advance that your board doesn't usually admit witnesses, if you think a witness would supply needed information and strengthen your case, you should ask the witness to attend with you. The board may admit him, or a refusal to hear the witness may show prejudice or unfairness on appeal or if the case ever gets to court.

If you plan to take a witness, select him carefully. If you want an occupational deferment, you will probably take your employer or supervisor. If you want a hardship-to-dependents deferment, you may want to take your dependent, a doctor who can testify about disability or family circumstances, a clergyman, social worker, employer, family friend, or neighbor. If you are a conscientious objector, you would take witnesses who know your character and sincerity, preferably from long acquaintance, and who may also know your religious beliefs and your feelings about war. In general, the best witness would be older than you and respected in the community—someone the board members would trust. Some boards have been willing to hear two or three, or even more witnesses, but this is rare.

Once the best witness has been selected and has agreed to attend, you and your witness should spend some time together talking about the process. Only the witness can decide what he will say, but you can help him understand what you are applying for and why, the purpose of the meeting, and the kind of information he will need to supply.

Any specific information the witness has should be put into letter form in advance and given to the board at the personal appearance. But the presence of the witness may still be valuable, for it gives the board members a chance to ask him questions and to evaluate his honesty and reliability. One of the Regulations on personal appearances states, "The registrant may present such further information as he believes will assist the local board in determining his proper classification" [REG 1624.2(b)]. It can be argued that the presence of the witness is the only way to show the board members that he is trustworthy, and therefore that refusing to allow witnesses would violate this provision of the Regulations.

The Regulations do not allow you to be represented or advised by a lawyer at the personal appearance [REG 1624.1(b)]. The courts have upheld this limitation, but some lawyers remain convinced it should be challenged and hope the courts will reverse their decisions. There is nothing to stop a lawyer from being admitted as a witness.

You may find it helpful to arrange for a group of friends to act as a "draft board" and put you through an advance "personal appearance." Some draft counselors will arrange for this role-play preparation because they believe it lets you experience some of the emotions of the actual personal appearance while you practice explaining your position.

At the Personal Appearance

It isn't possible to know how soon after your request the personal appearance will actually take place. Usually the clerk will send you a letter asking you to come to the board's next monthly meeting, but sometimes it may be several months before a board will schedule it. Some boards prefer to delay the personal appearance until after you have received your pre-induction physical examination. However long it takes, no induction order can be issued to you during the time allowed to request a personal appearance or appeal or while you are waiting for it [REG 1624.3]. For this reason, if you want to gain as much time as possible, you may mail your request for the personal appearance toward the end of your 30-day period.

If transportation problems or a personal emergency should keep you from attending your personal appearance, you should write to the board as quickly as possible explaining what happened and asking for a new appointment. If the reason is good, the local board should schedule a new personal appearance.

When the personal appearance actually takes place, you may meet with the entire board, some of its members, or only one member [REG 1624.2(a)]. Of course, if a majority of the members isn't present, no decision can legally be made at that time [REG 1604.56], but those present can talk with you and report to the others at a later meeting. The clerk may or may not be present. Sometimes the clerk or one of the board members takes notes of the meeting; you may be asked to sign these "official" notes to acknowledge that they are accurate (if they are, there is no harm in your signing if you wish to, but otherwise you should politely decline and promise to send your own summary).

You and all witnesses are required to swear (or affirm) that you will tell the truth [REG 1604.57].

The personal appearance may last only a few minutes, or may continue for half an hour or in rare cases even an hour. Some boards ask many questions; others merely allow you to make a statement. You should be prepared for anything. If you have brought the brief outline of your arguments suggested above, it will help you give a concise statement explaining why you should get the classification you want. If the board controls the discussion with questions, you may want to check off on your outline each of your arguments as you get the chance to make it. If you find the meeting is ending before you have said everything you consider important, you should ask permission to add a final statement. Some boards ask you if you have additional comments to make before they end the personal appearance.

It is sometimes useful to ask the board members some questions, if you can do so in a diplomatic way. "Have you read the letter from Mr._____?" may tell you how well they know your claim; if they haven't, you should summarize its contents. This may cause them to read your file more closely. "What would you consider sufficient evidence—or a suitable situation—to give the _____ classification?" may tell you on what basis the board grants the classification you want, and perhaps enable you to provide the needed information. It may even reveal whether the board is making decisions on an illegal basis.

Following the personal appearance, the local board must

consider all the evidence and place you in the lowest classification it believes you qualify for (using the order shown on page xvi).

Some boards vote immediately and tell you the result before you leave. Others dismiss you and vote in private. .

In either case, the local board *must* send you a new classification card after the personal appearance [REG 1624.2(d)]. This gives you official notice of the decision and starts a new 30-day period during which you can appeal.

After the Personal Appearance

Immediately after the personal appearance, you should write down everything that happened there, in dialogue form if possible. Your witness, if one was admitted, can help you remember, and can write about the part in which he participated. This summary should be as complete as memory allows, written in an objective, factual way. If your rights seem to have been violated by anything the board did or said, or failed to do, this should be included. At the end of the summary, or in a cover letter, you should ask the board to notify you if the summary has any inaccuracies. You should send your summary, and any prepared by witnesses, to the local board for your permanent file. In this way, although no transcript of the meeting is made, you can create a record which may aid you if you later need to complain of unfairness to the appeal board or state director, or to defend yourself in court. And at the same time you fulfill your obligation to summarize in writing any new information you give at the personal appearance [REG 1624.2(b), LBM 52].

APPEAL

You have the right to appeal within 30 days after the board mails you a new classification card following the personal appearance (60 days if you are in a foreign country, other than Canada or Mexico). Or, if you don't use your right to a personal appearance, you can appeal when you receive the original classification or reclassification. All that is necessary is a letter to the local board saying, "I request an appeal," with your Selective Service number, the date, and your signature; usually the letter should go on to explain why you feel you should receive the classification you want.

You aren't the only one with the right to appeal your classification. An employer who has requested an occupational deferment for you must be notified of the board's decision at the same time as you are, and he has the right to appeal whether you do or not. Similarly, anyone who claims to be your dependent has the right to appeal. Three officials of the Selective Service System also have this power—the government appeal agent for the local board, the state director, and the national director—and they may sometimes appeal when the local board gives you a classification which you want but which they disagree with.

It is a good idea if you are appealing to try to find out why your previous efforts have been unsuccessful. This may be difficult. A few local boards will answer a letter asking why the requested classification wasn't given, but most will not. Sometimes the clerk knows. This is a good time to see the government appeal agent again, for he may be able to find out why the local board didn't give the desired classification in response to the written request and the personal appearance.

If these efforts give clues to the evidence needed, it should be obtained if possible and mailed to the local board with your request for an appeal. If you are submitting important new evidence with your request for an appeal, ask the local board to review the file before sending it to the appeal board; the board may decide to give you the classification you want on the basis of the new evidence.

Even if you have written to request an appeal early in the 30-day period, the Regulations seem to require that your file be kept at the local board until this period is over, then sent to the appeal board within five days [REG 1626.14], but boards often don't wait. Thus you should have 30 days to try to get evidence that will convince the appeal board, but you would be wise to act as quickly as possible.

Unlike personal appearances, some appeals can be transferred. If you are working or living in a different appeal board area, your appeal letter may ask that the appeal be sent to the appeal board there instead of the one in your local board area. This seems especially useful in appeals for occupational deferments, or in cases where you believe you will be the victim of prejudice in your home area. The transfer must be allowed on request if you work in a different area and are applying for occupational deferment, or if you live in a different area regardless of the classification you want [REG 1626.11(b) and (c)].

The appeal board considers only the written information in your file and its own knowledge of "economic, industrial, and social conditions" in the area. It does not allow you to appear before it, nor does it do any investigation of its own. If it feels more information is needed, however, it can send the file back to the local board to get the information and then return it [REG 1626.23], but this is not often done.

After considering all the information in the file, the appeal board must place you in the lowest classification it believes you are eligible for (using the order on page xvi). It sends its decision, including its vote, to the local board, which mails a new classification card to you. Thus you know the appeal board's decision and whether you can appeal further, for only a split vote in the appeal board allows you the right to a Presidential appeal, and split votes are rare.

AFTER AN UNSUCCESSFUL APPEAL

Reconsideration by Appeal Board

In cases where the state appeal board vote is unanimous, you cannot appeal to the Presidential board, but there are several steps open to you.

The first of these is to try to get the state appeal board to reconsider its decision. The Regulations provide that it must reconsider on request of the state or national director of Selective Service, and they give the government appeal agent for the local board specific power to ask the state director to issue such a request [REG 1626.61].

If you believe your classification by the appeal board was unjust, you should act immediately. First, you should write to the state director (addresses are on page 279), stating why the reconsideration should be allowed and explaining in detail why it is "in the national interest or necessary to avoid an unjustice." You should enclose copies of a few of your most convincing items of evidence. You should write to both state directors if your local board is in one state and your appeal was transferred to another. Second, you should arrange a meeting with the government appeal agent and urge him to ask the state director to have the appeal board reconsider its decision.

It is a good idea to send the national director a carbon copy of the letter to the state director and copies of the evidence enclosed with it, along with a cover letter telling him that he is being kept informed in case his help is needed later. Then, if the state director refuses to request the reconsideration, the national director should be asked to do so.

Presidential Appeal

Those few registrants who receive split votes at the state

appeal board level have a right to a Presidential appeal. You must request it in writing within 30 days after the local board mails the classification card with the result of the state appeal (no longer period is allowed for those who are in foreign countries), although the local board may allow the appeal after 30 days if it is convinced you didn't understand your right to appeal or that your delay was due to a cause beyond your control.

But there is also another way the Presidential appeal can be obtained. The state and national directors have the right to order it at any time regardless of the vote of the appeal board [REG 1627.1], and the government appeal agent has the right to ask the state director to use this power, provided no induction order has been issued [REG 1626.61]. Therefore, if your request was denied by unanimous vote of the appeal board, but you want a Presidential appeal because you feel the decision was unjust, you should follow the same steps mentioned above for trying to get the appeal board to reconsider. This advice applies equally if the reconsideration is not granted, or if the appeal board has reconsidered but still denies the request unanimously.

Since the local board is free to issue an induction order as soon as a unanimous state appeal board decision has been mailed to you, provided you have already passed a pre-induction physical examination, great haste is sometimes necessary at this point. The following steps may be taken:

1. Write to the state director asking him to request that the appeal board reconsider its decision or to make a Presidential appeal, and enclose convincing evidence.

2. At the same time, see the government appeal agent and ask him to make both requests of the state director.

3. Keep the national director informed, and if the state

director refuses to act, ask the national director for the appeal board reconsideration or the Presidential appeal.

4. Send the local board copies of all letters as they are sent and ask it by letter to postpone issuance of an induction order until the directors decide whether to act.

Even if an induction order is issued while the state and national directors are considering whether to act, it will automatically be canceled if one of them agrees to allow a reconsideration or a Presidential appeal.

If a Presidential appeal is allowed, the file is reviewed by the three-member National Selective Service Appeal Board, which does not meet you. Like the lower boards, the Presidential board must put you in the lowest classification it believes you qualify for. It returns the file to your local board, which mails you a classification card showing the decision of the Presidential board.

There is, of course, no further appeal possible after the Presidential appeal, but even so you may not have reached the end of the process. If you can provide evidence that you qualify for a different classification, or get very significant and entirely new evidence for the classification you were denied, you may be able to get the local board to reopen your classification, which would allow you to start the entire process over again.

If your rights seem to have been violated or strong evidence has been unreasonably ignored, and if no Selective Service official will act to correct the situation, as a final resort you may wish to write to your Congressman and Senators.

Sometimes an experienced draft counselor or an attorney familiar with Selective Service can see possibilities you may have overlooked.

CHAPTER SIX

EXAMINATION AND INDUCTION

There are two final steps by which you are drafted into military service: an examination to determine whether you are eligible, and induction into the armed forces. (Chapter 15 deals with the alternative forms of service for conscientious objectors.)

ARMED FORCES PHYSICAL EXAMINATION

You may not be ordered into military service by your draft board unless you have previously taken, passed, and been officially notified of passing an armed forces physical examination.

There are only two exceptions. If you have been declared delinquent (discussed in Chapter 7) or if you have volunteered for induction (discussed in Chapter 8), you may be ordered for induction without previous physical examination [REG 1628.10], but you must be given the full examination at the time of induction; you will be rejected if you fail it.

Most men are examined shortly before the board expects to draft them. A local board may order registrants to take their physical examinations whenever they are classified as eligible for service (I-A, I-A-O, or I-O), regardless of whether an appeal is pending, starting with those closest to being drafted [REG 1628.11(b)]. A board may also order a man in any other classification to take this examination "if it determines that his induction may shortly occur" [REG 1628.11(c)].

When an Order to Report for Armed Forces Physical Examination (Form 223) is issued, you are required to obey it unless you get it postponed or canceled, or transferred to a different city.

The conscientious objector classified I-O is the only exception. He may take the physical examination if he wishes, but will be ordered to perform civilian work anyway if he doesn't take the examination. The I-O registrant may wish to take the examination if he expects to be disqualified, for then he isn't required to do civilian work.

A local board is allowed to postpone the date of your physical examination for up to 60 days in case of a death in your family, extreme family emergency, serious illness, or other emergency, and one additional 60-day postponement is possible if the emergency makes it necessary. In addition, the state and national directors of Selective Service have unlimited authority to allow postponements for any reason [REG 1628.12].

The Regulations don't provide for or prohibit canceling an order to take a physical examination, but both logic and the national director [see LBM 66, for example] suggest that it can be canceled by the local board which issued it, especially if it seems to have been issued in error, as when the local board has ordered you examined while you are deferred and there is no likelihood that your deferment will end soon.

The Regulations do not state how much time you must be given from the time the Order to Report for Armed Forces Physical Examination is mailed until the date set for the examination, but it seems logical to assume that at least 10 days' notice should be allowed, as is provided for an induction order [REG 1632.1]. In practice, the order is usually mailed two to four weeks before the date of the examination.

Approval Not Required.

SELECTIVE SERVICE SYSTEM

ORDER TO REPORT FOR ARMED FORCES PHYSICAL EXAMINATION

(Local Board Stamp)

(Date of mailing)

SELECTIVE SERVICE NO.

You are hereby directed to present yourself for Armed Forces Physical Examination by reporting

at:

To

at: _____
(Place of reporting)

on _____ at _____
(Date)   (Hour)

_____
(Member, Executive Secretary or clerk of Local Board)

IMPORTANT NOTICE
(Read Each Paragraph Carefully)

TO ALL REGISTRANTS:

When you report pursuant to this order you will be forwarded to an Armed Forces Examining Station where it will be determined whether you are qualified for military service under current standards. Upon completion of your examination, you will be returned to the place of reporting designated above. It is possible that you may be retained at the Examining Station for more than 1 day for the purpose of further testing or for medical consultation. You will be furnished transportation, and meals and lodging when necessary, from the place of reporting designated above to the Examining Station and return. Following your examination your local board will mail you a statement issued by the commanding officer of the station showing whether you are qualified for military service under current standards.

If you are employed, you should inform your employer of this order and that the examination is merely to determine whether you are qualified for military service. To protect your right to return to your job, you must report for work as soon as possible after the completion of your examination. You may jeopardize your reemployment rights if you do not report for work at the beginning of your next regularly scheduled working period after you have returned to your place of employment.

IF YOU HAVE HAD PREVIOUS MILITARY SERVICE, OR ARE NOW A MEMBER OF THE NATIONAL GUARD OR A RESERVE COMPONENT OF THE ARMED FORCES, BRING EVIDENCE WITH YOU. IF YOU WEAR GLASSES, BRING THEM. IF YOU HAVE ANY PHYSICAL OR MENTAL CONDITION WHICH, IN YOUR OPINION, MAY DISQUALIFY YOU FOR SERVICE IN THE ARMED FORCES, BRING A PHYSICIAN'S CERTIFICATE DESCRIBING THAT CONDITION, IF NOT ALREADY FURNISHED TO YOUR LOCAL BOARD.

If you are so far from your own Local Board that reporting in compliance with this Order will be a hardship and you desire to report to the Local Board in the area in which you are now located, take this Order and go immediately to that Local Board and make written request for transfer for examination.

TO CLASS I-A AND I-A-O REGISTRANTS:

If you fail to report for examination as directed, you may be declared delinquent and ordered to report for induction into the Armed Forces. You will also be subject to fine and imprisonment under the provisions of the Military Selective Service Act of 1967.

TO CLASS I-O REGISTRANTS:

This examination is given for the purpose of determining whether you are qualified for military service. If you are found qualified, you will be available, in lieu of induction, to be ordered to perform civilian work contributing to the maintenance of the national health, safety or interest. If you fail to report for or to submit to this examination, you will be subject to be ordered to perform civilian work in the same manner as if you had taken the examination and had been found qualified for military service.

SSS Form 223 (Revised 6-20-68) (Previous printings may be used until exhausted.)

73

Transfer

If you are ordered to report for a physical examination in the city where your local board is, but you are then so far away that reporting there would be a "hardship," you may transfer the order to a local board where you are. You merely take the order to the nearby local board and fill out a transfer form there, indicating the reason why you are away from your local board area. The Regulations require you to do this "immediately" [REG 1628.14(b)], but in practice transfers seem to be allowed without dispute up to the date set for the original examination, and sometimes even after. The local board to which you go is supposed to "investigate the circumstances of the registrant's absence from his own local board area" and allow the transfer only if you have a "good reason for [your] absence" and if it believes returning would be a real hardship [REG 1628.14(c) and (d)]. In practice, transfers are routinely allowed and no investigation seems to be made.

When an examination is transferred, the nearby board must get your papers from your own local board and then order you to report the next time it is sending men for examination. Most boards do so only once a month. As a result, a delay may occur, sometimes of three to six weeks, before your examination takes place.

The Examination

Physical examinations are given by the Army, not the Selective Service System. They take place at Armed Forces Examining and Entrance Stations (AFEES), generally buildings in the centers of major cities but occasionally on Army bases. Transportation is provided or paid by Selective Service, and meals and lodging are provided if the examination takes long enough to require any.

Since the AFEES examines large numbers of men each day, and since the doctors, orderlies, and clerks assigned there must process them in assembly-line fashion as quickly as possible, the examinations are often careless. If you believe you have a medical or other condition which should disqualify you, bring letters and other evidence from your own doctors and insist that they be read and that your condition be carefully evaluated. Chapter 13 gives detailed suggestions for insuring full consideration of medical and other grounds for rejection.

In rare cases, when extended examination is necessary, the AFEES may require you to stay there or go to a military hospital for up to three days, or to return at a later time.

You should be told before you leave the AFEES whether or not you have been found acceptable for military service [AR 601-270, 27]. If they don't tell you, you may wish to ask, pointing out the requirement that you be told. However, you must also receive an official notification from your local board. It sends you a Statement of Acceptability (DD Form 62) indicating whether you were found acceptable or unacceptable. As soon as this form is mailed to you, an induction order may be issued, though the day of induction must be at least 21 days after the form was mailed [REG 1631.7(a)].

There is no official provision for appealing the decision that you are acceptable, unless it results in a change of classification—as from I-Y to I-A—in which case you have the usual personal appearance and appeal rights described in Chapter 5. Unofficial appeal procedures are discussed in Chapter 13.

INDUCTION

An induction order requires you to report for military

STATEMENT OF ACCEPTABILITY

☆ U. S. GOVERNMENT PRINTING OFFICE: 1966—222-921

LAST NAME - FIRST NAME - MIDDLE NAME

PRESENT HOME ADDRESS

SELECTIVE SERVICE NUMBER

LOCAL BOARD ADDRESS

THE QUALIFICATIONS OF THE ABOVE-NAMED REGISTRANT HAVE BEEN CONSIDERED IN ACCORDANCE WITH THE CURRENT REGULATIONS GOVERNING ACCEPTANCE OF SELECTIVE SERVICE REGISTRANTS AND HE WAS THIS DATE:

☐ 1. FOUND FULLY ACCEPTABLE FOR INDUCTION INTO THE ARMED FORCES.

☐ 2. FOUND NOT ACCEPTABLE FOR INDUCTION UNDER CURRENT STANDARDS.

DATE

PLACE

TYPED OR STAMPED NAME AND GRADE OF JOINT EXAMINING AND INDUCTION STATION COMMANDER

SIGNATURE

DD FORM 62
1 MAR 59

PREVIOUS EDITIONS OF THIS FORM ARE OBSOLETE.

REGISTRANT COPY 2

Any inquiry relative to personal status should be referred to your Local Board

76

service. It can be issued by the local board only when *all* of these requirements are met:

1. You are classified I-A or I-A-O.

2. You don't have any further right to appeal. (It can't be issued during the 30-day period after a classification is given by the local board, or while an appeal is in process.)

3. The file is at the local board. (Thus if the government appeal agent has sent the file to the state director, or the state or national director has sent for it, to consider allowing an appeal board reconsideration or a Presidential appeal, no induction order can be issued.)

4. You have taken and passed a pre-induction physical examination and have been notified officially on the Statement of Acceptability (except for delinquents and volunteers for induction, discussed at the beginning of this chapter.)

5. The local board has no registrants available to meet its current quota who are higher than you in draft eligibility.

Order of Draft Eligibility

In determining draft eligibility for the last requirement, local boards must follow this order under present Regulations [REG 1631.7(a)]:

1. Delinquents aged 19 or over, *oldest* first.

2. Volunteers for induction under 26 years old, in order of volunteering.

3. Unmarried men and men married after August 26, 1965, aged 19 through 25, *oldest* first.

4. Men married by August 26, 1965, and who still live with their wives, aged 19 through 25, *oldest* first.

5. Men aged 26 through 34 with "extended liability" because they have received deferments, *youngest* first.

6. Men aged 18½ to 19, *oldest* first.

Because local boards must draft in this order, and because there have always been enough men in the first three or four groups to fill draft calls, men in the last two groups have not been inducted since the present draft system began in 1948. (Doctors, dentists, and other medical specialists are the only exceptions to this; under special rules, they are drafted through age 34.) It is extremely unlikely that any man who has reached 26, and who is not a delinquent or subject to the doctors' draft, could ever be drafted except in an emergency which produced draft calls far higher than those of the Korean and Vietnam wars. Thus, in practice, the "extended liability" to age 35, which any registrant receives if he has ever had a deferment, means very little under present conditions.

However, this could be changed for college students by one unused provision of the 1967 draft law, designed to allow drafting 19-year-olds first. This law gives the Secretary of Defense power to declare a "prime age group" from which local boards would draft men as soon as they ran out of delinquents and volunteers. The "prime age group" would be all I-A and I-A-O registrants born in the calendar year named by the Secretary, plus all I-A and I-A-O registrants who have ever received a I-S(C) classification or who have requested and received a II-S classification since June 30, 1967. These former students would go into the "prime age group" regardless of their actual age until they reached 35. If a "prime age group" is ever formed, those in it will presumably be drafted in birthday order (starting with those born in

January). These details are far from definite, for the law is vague [MSSA 6(h)(1), REG 1631.7(b)]. In any case, no "prime age group" has been formed or publicly announced at this writing, and it is unlikely that this provision will ever be used as it stands. It is, however, a possibility which those who receive student deferments must consider.

Induction Order

When you are near enough to the top of your local board's eligibility list to be needed for its current draft quota, you are issued an Order to Report for Induction (Form 252). As mentioned above, the date to report must be at least 21 days after the mailing of your Statement of Acceptability. In addition, the order must be mailed at least 10 days before the date you are to report.

An induction order can be postponed or transferred under exactly the same conditions as an order to report for a pre-induction physical examination, discussed at the beginning of this chapter. In addition, recent law school graduates may get their induction dates postponed to allow them to take the next bar examination [LBM 44], and in some states a similar arrangement is made for other professional examinations. For students who receive induction orders during a school year, see page 126.

When the local board issues the induction order, you no longer have the right to have your classification reopened because of changed circumstances or new information (except in the cases discussed on page 56), nor can the government appeal agent take action to get your classification considered further. However, the state and national directors have the right to reopen or appeal a classification at any time, and any induction order would automatically be canceled if this power were used. And presumably the local board which issued an induction order has the power to

☆ U.S. GOVERNMENT PRINTING OFFICE: 1968—292—610

A

Approval Not Required.

SELECTIVE SERVICE SYSTEM
ORDER TO REPORT FOR INDUCTION

(LOCAL BOARD STAMP)

(Date of mailing)

SELECTIVE SERVICE NO.

The President of the United States,

To ....

GREETING:

You are hereby ordered for induction into the Armed Forces of the United States, and to report

at .... (Place of reporting)

on .... at ....
   (Date)   (Hour)

for forwarding to an Armed Forces Induction Station.

....
(Member, Executive Secretary, or clerk of Local Board

80

IMPORTANT NOTICE
(Read Each Paragraph Carefully)

IF YOU HAVE HAD PREVIOUS MILITARY SERVICE, OR ARE NOW A MEMBER OF THE NATIONAL GUARD OR A RESERVE COMPONENT OF THE ARMED FORCES, BRING EVIDENCE WITH YOU. IF YOU WEAR GLASSES, BRING THEM. IF MARRIED, BRING PROOF OF YOUR MARRIAGE. IF YOU HAVE ANY PHYSICAL OR MENTAL CONDITION WHICH, IN YOUR OPINION, MAY DISQUALIFY YOU FOR SERVICE IN THE ARMED FORCES, BRING A PHYSICIAN'S CERTIFICATE DESCRIBING THAT CONDITION, IF NOT ALREADY FURNISHED TO YOUR LOCAL BOARD.

Valid documents are required to substantiate dependency claims in order to receive basic allowance for quarters. Be sure to take the following with you when reporting to the induction station. The documents will be returned to you. (*a*) FOR LAWFUL WIFE OR LEGITIMATE CHILD UNDER 21 YEARS OF AGE—original, certified copy or photostat of a certified copy of marriage certificate, child's birth certificate, or a public or church record of marriage issued over the signature and seal of the custodian of the church or public records; (*b*) FOR LEGALLY ADOPTED CHILD—certified court order of adoption; (*c*) FOR CHILD OF DIVORCED SERVICE MEMBER (Child in custody of person other than claimant)—(1) Certified or photostatic copies of receipts from custodian of child evidencing serviceman's contributions for support, and (2) Divorce decree, court support order or separation order; (*d*) FOR DEPENDENT PARENT—affidavits establishing that dependency.

Bring your Social Security Account Number Card. If you do not have one, apply at nearest Social Security Administration Office. If you have life insurance, bring a record of the insurance company's address and your policy number. Bring enough clean clothes for 3 days. Bring enough money to last 1 month for personal purchases.

This Local Board will furnish transportation, and meals and lodging when necessary, from the place of reporting to the induction station where you will be examined. If found qualified, you will be inducted into the Armed Forces. If found not qualified, return transportation and meals and lodging when necessary, will be furnished to the place of reporting.

You may be found not qualified for induction. Keep this in mind in arranging your affairs, to prevent any undue hardship if you are not inducted. If employed, inform your employer of this possibility. Your employer can then be prepared to continue your employment if you are not inducted. To protect your right to return to your job if you are not inducted, you must report for work as soon as possible after the completion of your induction examination. You may jeopardize your reemployment rights if you do not report for work at the beginning of your next regularly scheduled working period after you have returned to your place of employment.

Willful failure to report at the place and hour of the day named in this Order subjects the violator to fine and imprisonment. Bring this Order with you when you report.

If you are so far from your own local board that reporting in compliance with this Order will be a serious hardship, go immediately to any local board and make written request for transfer of your delivery for induction, taking this Order with you.

SSS Form 252 (Revised 4-28-65)   (Previous printings may be used until exhausted.)

81

cancel it if it was improperly issued, as when the wrong order of eligibility was followed, although the Regulations do not deal with this question.

If your pre-induction physical examination was more than a year before the date of induction, you must receive another complete examination at the time of induction; if it was more recent, you receive a less complete "physical inspection" at the time of induction [AR 601-270, 68 and 69]. If the examination or inspection reveals a disqualifying condition, you will be rejected and sent home, and later be reclassified by your local board.

If you are found still qualified, you are immediately inducted into the armed forces—usually the Army, but occasionally the Marines. The other services very rarely use draftees.

The actual induction consists of a brief ceremony in which you are told that you are about to enter military service and that you must take one step forward when your name and branch of service are announced. If you take the step forward, you are in the armed forces and subject to military law, whether or not you take the oath of allegiance, which is given later [AR 601-270, 37].

If you refuse to take the step forward, even after warnings and repeated chances, you are considered to have refused induction and are reported to Selective Service for prosecution [AR 601-270, 40c]. You are asked to sign papers acknowledging that you have refused induction, but you are not required to sign them. In most cases you are allowed to leave to await later arrest, but in New York City (Whitehall Street) you will probably be arrested immediately. If you wish to challenge your classification in court by refusing induction, you will probably be advised by your attorney to cooperate with the process up to the point of stepping forward. If you hope for a successful court test, you should consult an attorney experienced in Selective Service cases before refusing induction, and preferably much earlier, as soon as it becomes likely that a court trial will take place.

CHAPTER SEVEN

TWO SPECIAL PROBLEMS—
TRAVEL ABROAD, DELINQUENCY

This chapter discusses two unrelated Selective Service provisions that affect relatively few registrants but that often create confusion and problems when they arise.

TRAVEL ABROAD

There is provision for a local board—or the state or national director—to issue a Permit for Registrant to Depart from the United States (Form 300) [REG 1621.16]. Many registrants and some draft boards believe it is illegal for a registrant to go abroad without this permit, but this is not true.

While called a "permit," it is more like an insurance policy against being bothered by your draft board while you are abroad for a specified period of time. It is a formal promise from Selective Service that your deferment will continue for the period for which the permit is used; or if you are not deferred, that no induction order will be issued for this period. It enables you to travel, work, or study abroad for a limited time with reasonable certainty that your draft board won't do anything that will force you to return early.

Most draft boards will issue the permit only if you don't need it, because they intend to take no action that would affect you during that period anyway. But some boards refuse to grant permits even then.

If you are deferred, it may be best simply to inform your

board in writing, just before your departure, telling it where you are going, when you will leave, and when you will return. Give an address or addresses abroad if you can, so the board will send any correspondence directly to you, and so you will have 60 days instead of 30 to appeal an unexpected reclassification (only 30 days if you are in Canada or Mexico).

If you request the permit and your request is denied, you can still leave the country and return perfectly legally even though your board may be annoyed with you.

Many students go abroad for the summer without informing their boards, relying upon parents to forward any mail promptly. Sometimes they leave signed letters requesting a personal appearance and appeal for their parents to mail to the board in case of a reclassification. So long as your board has a mailing address this is perfectly legal, but we advise sending the board your overseas address. Your parents may forget, or a personal appearance may be scheduled before you can return.

If you are I-A, I-A-O, or I-O, and therefore in a position to be ordered to a pre-induction physical, or to induction or civilian work, it is best to apply for the permit. Physicals can sometimes be taken abroad [LBM 69], but this may be difficult to arrange and you may have to pay for your own transportation to an Army base. Boards have been known to delay the processing of registrants who have an opportunity to travel abroad for several weeks, and yours might be that kind of board. The same applies if you are awaiting a personal appearance, or the results of an appeal.

Undergraduate exchange students should receive the II-S deferment if their year abroad gives them full credit toward their degree.

The permit is not relevant to registrants who emigrate (see Chapters 16 and 17).

Form approved.
Budget Bureau No. 33.R106.4.

(LOCAL BOARD STAMP)

SELECTIVE SERVICE SYSTEM

PERMIT FOR REGISTRANT TO DEPART FROM THE UNITED STATES

1. NAME OF REGISTRANT

_____ _____ _____
(First)   (Middle)   (Last)

2. SELECTIVE SERVICE NO.

4. CLASSIFICATION

3. PRESENT ADDRESS

_____ _____ _____
(Number and Street) (City or town) (State) (Zip Code)

5. PLACE OF BIRTH

6. DATE OF BIRTH

_____ _____ _____
(City or town)   (State)   (Country)

7. IF NONCITIZEN, ALIEN REGISTRATION NUMBER _____

8. IN HIS APPLICATION THE REGISTRANT GAVE THE FOLLOWING INFORMATION:

A. COUNTRIES TO BE VISITED

(Date) _____

86

B. ORGANIZATIONS OR INDIVIDUALS REPRESENTED

C. NATURE OF BUSINESS

The above-named registrant is hereby authorized to depart from the United States and to remain absent therefrom until _____
(Date)

_____
(Signature)

_____
(Title)

NOTICE: Before leaving the United States, if an alien, secure a reentry permit, if necessary, from the Immigration and Naturalization Service, Department of Justice.

SSS Form 300 (Revised 1-29-65)   (Previous printings are obsolete)

U.S. GOVERNMENT PRINTING OFFICE 1965 OF—762–886

87

DRAFT DELINQUENCY

"A 'delinquent' is a person required to be registered under the selective service law who fails or neglects to perform any duty required of him under the provisions of the selective service law" [REG 1602.4]. Thus anyone who has broken any of the draft rules can be declared delinquent. Of course, you could be prosecuted for the violation, tried in federal court, and if found guilty sentenced to a maximum of 5 years in prison or a $10,000 fine, or both [MSSA 12].

However, the Regulations provide an alternative form of punishment, not mentioned in the law. They allow the local board to declare you delinquent by sending you a form notifying you of this and telling you why. The board also can reclassify you into a classification eligible for service (I-A, I-A-O, or I-O, depending on whether it believes you are a conscientious objector), and order you into the appropriate form of service ahead of all other registrants.

The delinquency process does not require the local board to hold any hearings or gather evidence, but the Regulations provide that you "may be removed from that status by the local board at any time" [REG 1642.4(c)]. Therefore, if you demonstrate that you haven't violated any regulation, or if you fulfill the obligation you had earlier neglected (for example, by taking a pre-induction physical you had previously missed, or supplying your current address) presumably you must be removed from the delinquency status. If you wish to protest a declaration of delinquency, it is often useful to ask the local board to allow you to attend a meeting to discuss it with them. The Regulations make no provision for appealing a declaration of delinquency, although some attorneys feel a "I-A Delinquent" is a different classification from "I-A" and should be appealed like any other reclassification.

When the delinquency results in a change of classification, clearly the usual rights of personal appearance and appeal exist, and a reopening of classification on the basis of new evidence or a change of circumstances is still possible [REG 1642.14]. No induction order may be issued while these rights are being used, so you may have the opportunity to contest your delinquency status. As indicated, if you are declared delinquent while already classified I-A, you presumably have no opportunity for a personal appearance or appeal, although your status has been significantly changed by the requirement that delinquents be inducted ahead of all other registrants, even volunteers.

It is important to note that you may be declared delinquent only if you violate a specific provision of the Selective Service Act or Regulations. Thus it is improper for a board to declare you delinquent for traveling abroad without permission from Selective Service (see first part of this chapter), or for refusing to answer the Armed Forces Security Questionnaire at a pre-induction physical examination (see Chapter 13), or even for insisting on passing out leaflets or giving speeches at the physical examination, since none of these acts is forbidden by the Selective Service law or Regulations. Local boards *have* declared men delinquent for each of these acts, evidently because they did not understand the limitations of this part of the Regulations.

At this writing, there are several dozen cases in court which center around the use of the delinquency provisions. With national Selective Service in open disagreement with the Department of Justice, it is difficult to predict the outcome. The courts may rule out the delinquency provisions altogether, on the grounds that Congress didn't authorize them in the law, or more likely may restrict the ways they can be used.

Approval
Not Required.

SELECTIVE SERVICE SYSTEM

DELINQUENCY NOTICE

To _____
      (First)   (Middle)   (Last)

Address _____
         (Street and Number or RFD Route)

_____
(City, Town, or Village)   (County)   (State)   (ZIP Code)

(Local Board Stamp)

_____
                    (Date Declared Delinquent)

_____
                    (Date of Mailing)

SELECTIVE SERVICE NO.

90

1. YOU ARE HEREBY NOTIFIED THAT THIS LOCAL BOARD HAS DECLARED YOU TO BE A DELINQUENT BECAUSE OF YOUR FAILURE TO PERFORM THE FOLLOWING DUTY OR DUTIES REQUIRED OF YOU UNDER THE SELECTIVE SERVICE LAW:

2. YOU ARE HEREBY DIRECTED TO REPORT TO THIS LOCAL BOARD IMMEDIATELY IN PERSON OR BY MAIL, OR TO TAKE THIS NOTICE TO THE LOCAL BOARD NEAREST YOU FOR ADVICE AS TO WHAT YOU SHOULD DO.

3. YOUR WILLFUL FAILURE TO PERFORM THE FOREGOING DUTY OR DUTIES IS A VIOLATION OF MILITARY SELECTIVE SERVICE ACT, OF 1967, WHICH IS PUNISHABLE BY IMPRISONMENT FOR AS MUCH AS 5 YEARS OR A FINE OF AS MUCH AS $10,000, OR BY BOTH SUCH FINE AND IMPRISONMENT. YOU MAY BE CLASSIFIED IN CLASS 1-A AS A DELINQUENT AND ORDERED TO REPORT FOR INDUCTION.

_____

(Member, Executive Secretary, or Clerk of Local Board)

INSTRUCTIONS

A Delinquency Notice (SSS Form 304) shall be prepared by the Local Board whenever it declares the registrant to be a delinquent because of his failure to perform any duty or duties required of him other than failure to comply with an Order to Report for Induction (SSS Form 252), or an Order to Report for Civilian Work and Statement of Employer (SSS Form 153). This notice shall be prepared in triplicate, and the specific duty or duties which the registrant has failed to perform shall be described in detail in the space provided. The Local Board shall (a) mail the original to the registrant at his last known address, (b) file a copy in the registrant's Cover Sheet (SSS Form 101), and (c) mail a copy to the State Director of Selective Service.

SSS Form 304 (5-25-65)

PART II

MILITARY AND NONMILITARY SERVICE

"The Congress further declares that in a free society the obligations and privileges of serving in the armed forces and the reserve components thereof shall be shared generally, in accordance with a system of selection which is fair and just, and which is consistent with the maintenance of an effective national economy."

MILITARY SELECTIVE SERVICE ACT OF 1967, 1(c)

CHAPTER EIGHT

MILITARY AND NONMILITARY SERVICE: I-C, I-D

If you perform military service, you will enter it in one of three ways (in addition to the noncombatant service for conscientious objectors discussed in Chapters 14 and 15):

1. Enlisting or applying for a commission—by volunteering directly for one of the branches of the armed forces.

2. Being inducted through Selective Service—by waiting until you are drafted in the normal order (discussed in Chapter 6), or volunteering for earlier induction.

3. Joining the reserves of one of the armed forces, including the National Guard and Coast Guard.

We will not try to explain all the choices open to you if you decide to serve in the armed forces. There are many choices, and they are constantly changing.

While on active duty, you are classified I-C by your draft board, though it does not send you a classification card. After active duty is completed, if you have served the required time, you are classified IV-A (discussed in Chapter 12).

ENLISTING

More than three out of every four men in the armed forces enter by voluntary enlistment or commissioning. Most of the openings in the Army are filled by enlistment, and the Marine

Corps, Navy, Air Force, and Coast Guard seldom or never take draftees. All of the branches prefer volunteers because the man who enlists is generally more strongly motivated to serve in the armed forces and is more likely to re-enlist, so the military gets more return for its investment in training.

Therefore, the military branches offer various incentives for enlisting. You may be promised training in the field you are interested in, or assignment overseas in the area of your choice, but these promises may not be kept if the program is closed or you don't meet the qualifications for it. Ordinarily you must sign up for three, four, or more years, although both the Navy and the Marines accept a limited number of two-year volunteers. In general, the longer you agree to serve, the more training you will receive.

Another advantage of enlisting is the chance to choose which branch of the armed forces you will enter.

The man who enlists, like the man who is drafted, must spend a total of six years in military service. Only part of the six years is on full-time, uniformed, active duty. The remainder is spent in the reserves. In general, unless you serve on active duty for five years or longer, you enter the Ready Reserve of your branch of service when you finish your active duty and remain in it until the last year or two years, when you are transferred to the Standby Reserve. In the Ready Reserve, you will probably have to attend weekly or monthly drill meetings, and often two weeks of summer camp. You can be called into active service with your unit in case of need. Thus you will probably not be free of a military obligation when you finish the number of years you volunteered for. Ready Reserve units have been called to active duty during the Vietnam buildup. Once you are transferred to the Standby Reserve, it is extremely unlikely that you will be called to active duty, and there are no training requirements.

If you enlist you will get the same pay (based on rank and number of dependents) and benefits as those who are drafted, and you will receive the same educational and other veterans benefits after you finish active duty, including the right to get your job back if you are still qualified for it.

There are basically three ways you can get a commission as an officer:

1. By graduating from one of the military academies.

2. By taking advanced R.O.T.C. in college.

3. By qualifying for Officer Candidate School. This possibility may be open to you after you have entered the armed forces, but it often means extending your length of service.

INDUCTION THROUGH SELECTIVE SERVICE

If you volunteer for induction, you are in precisely the same situation as the man who is drafted. You are required to serve two years in the Army, and you have no choices of training and location. The only advantage of volunteering for induction is getting it over with, ending the wait to be drafted.

To volunteer for induction, you apply through your local board (with parents' written permission if you are under 18). Usually the board will issue an induction order as soon as possible, whether or not you have taken a pre-induction physical examination; if you haven't, you will get a complete examination at the time of induction. Sometimes you are first sent for a pre-induction examination, then inducted if you pass it.

Any man 17 years old through 25 can volunteer for induction through his local board. However, you may be turned down if your board considers you eligible for

SELECTIVE SERVICE SYSTEM

Form Approved.
Budget Bureau No. 33–R122.5.

APPLICATION FOR VOLUNTARY INDUCTION

(Stamp of the local board of jurisdiction)

(Stamp of local board at which application is
filed if other than local board of jurisdiction)

I hereby apply for voluntary induction into the Armed Forces of the United States under the provisions of the Military Selective Service Act of 1967. For this purpose, I waive all rights of personal appearance and appeal if I am classified as available for service, and I consent to my induction at any time convenient to the Government. I understand that I may not be ordered to report for a preinduction armed forces physical examination, but that I may be ordered to report to an Armed Forces Induction Station for immediate induction. I am also aware of the possibility that I may be found not qualified for induction into the Armed Forces.

_____
(Applicant's Signature)

_____
(Date of Application)

DESCRIPTION OF APPLICANT

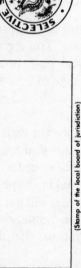

1. Name of applicant

_____   _____   _____
(First)   (Middle)   (Last)

2. Selective Service No.

98

3. Present mailing address

_____
(Number and street or R.F.D. Route)   (City, Town, or Village)   (County)   (State)   (Zip Code)

4. Number and address of local board where registered

5. Date of birth	6. Place of birth

7. If you were ever found not qualified for service in the Armed Forces, state (a) when _____
(b) where _____

CONSENT WHEN APPLICANT IS UNDER 18 YEARS OF AGE

I/we hereby certify that the above applicant has no other legal guardian than me/us and I/we do hereby consent to his induction into the Armed Forces of the United States under the provisions of the Military Selective Service Act of 1967. I/we understand that he may be assigned to overseas duty immediately upon completion of the required period of training.

_____   _____
(Other Parent, when required)   (Strike out one)   Parent or Legal Guardian

_____   _____
(Address)   (Address)

_____   _____
(Date)   (Date)

All entries must be typewritten or printed except signatures. The consent must be signed by both parents if living or by the surviving parent except that when another person is the legal guardian the consent must be signed by such guardian.

SSS Form 254 (Revised 10-29-64) (Previous printings may be used.)   GPO 927-836

99

deferment in II-A (occupational), II-C (agricultural), III-A (fathers and hardship-to-dependents), or IV-B (elected officials and judges).

The only advantage of waiting to be drafted, instead of enlisting or volunteering for induction, is delaying military service as long as possible. Your circumstances may change while you are waiting, and you may qualify for a classification which will allow you to avoid military service entirely, if that is your desire. On the other hand, delay may be a disadvantage, for it may mean interrupting your career, education, or family life at a much less convenient time.

JOINING THE RESERVES

Each branch of the armed forces has a variety of programs which allow you to spend your entire six-year period in the Ready Reserve except for a few months spent in full-time training, usually soon after you enlist. Each state has National Guard programs with similar requirements.

The "active duty for training" lasts from four months to three years, depending on your branch of service and the specialization you are trained for. When it is over, you are required to spend the remainder of the six years in the Ready Reserve, usually training once a week or once a month and for two weeks each summer. You remain subject to call-up to active duty at the order of the President. National Guard members can be called up by the governor of the state as well.

Many men think getting into the reserves will keep them from having to be away from home and job once the training period is finished. This is often true, and it is the reason most reserve units have long waiting lists. But, as mentioned above, reserve units have been called to active duty during 1968. In some cases they remain in the United States to replace military units being sent overseas, and in other cases they go overseas, either as a unit or divided up, with members assigned individually.

The attraction of the reserve programs is the chance of a short active-duty period and relative safety from being sent into combat. But you should consider the disadvantages as well. Your unit may be activated at any time, and in the case of the National Guard it may be called into service to deal with a natural disaster or to put down a riot. You will probably have to spend evenings or weekends for years in regular drill meetings and up to five summer vacations in training camp. And there is a widespread feeling among reservists that their training is both militarily worthless and of no value in civilian life, and that the time is therefore wasted.

Your draft board will classify you I-D during the time you are in the reserves or National Guard, including time spent in "active duty for training." When you have completed the required time, you are classified IV-A (discussed in Chapter 12). If your participation is considered unsatisfactory, you may be called to punitive active duty for 45 days. More often, you will be removed from the reserve unit and assigned to active duty for two years, less time already served. Or you may be turned over to your draft board for immediate induction and must spend a full two years in the Army. One of these steps is often taken if you miss more than 10% of the required drill meetings.

You will also be classified I-D while you are in certain military training programs. These include the senior divisions (normally the last two years) of the Army's college R.O.T.C. program and equivalent programs of the other services, provided you have agreed to accept a commission as an officer and to perform active duty when you graduate. This classification also is given to students in military colleges approved by the Secretary of Defense [listed in LBM 45], and to aviation cadets.

Few draft counselors have detailed information about the military alternatives. For this type of advice, you can often get current information from recruiters, though they will tend to try to sell their own branches of service. Naturally, as salesmen they will emphasize the advantages and challenges but say little about the frustrations and problems. Most of them know much more about active duty than about the reserves. Usually the best way to get information about reserve units is to visit those in your area and talk with men in them.

DISCHARGES AND TRANSFERS

In general, if you enter military service in any of these ways you must stay in until your term is over. However, each branch of the armed forces allows earlier discharges and transfers under certain conditions—subject to its judgment and convenience.

If your family circumstances change while you are on active duty and you are able to show that your dependents will suffer extreme hardship if you remain on active duty, you may be able to get a discharge or a transfer to duty near your home. The Red Cross may be able to help you verify the facts and apply for discharge.

If you develop a physical or mental disability, you may be eligible for a medical discharge. The conditions serious enough to warrant medical discharge from the armed forces are listed in Chapter 3 of Army Regulation 40-501. It may be helpful to get letters from civilian doctors in addition to seeing military doctors.

If you are in the Ready Reserve and you are working in a

field considered vital to the civilian economy, or are a college senior or graduate student preparing to enter such a field [listed in LBM 79], you may be transferred to the Standby Reserve, provided you are not judged to have a "critical military skill." You may also be transferred to the Standby Reserve if recalling you to active duty would cause your family extreme hardship.

If, while on active or reserve duty, you become conscientiously opposed to participation in war, you may be transferred to noncombatant duty, often medical service. If you are opposed even to this, you may be discharged. The requirements for transfer and discharge as a conscientious objector (CO) are the same as for Selective Service classifications I-A-O and I-O, discussed in Chapters 14 and 15. However, there are two important differences. First, your conscientious objection must have crystallized *after* you entered military service. A man classified I-A-O may apply for discharge as a CO, however, if his conscientious position has clearly changed. And second, it is extremely hard to achieve recognition as a CO within the armed forces. Before the middle of 1966, about 60% to 80% of applications for CO discharge were approved; since then, an estimated 4% of applications have been approved by the Army, with somewhat higher approval rates in the other services. However, new procedures started in 1968 are improving the chances of being discharged as a CO.

Applications for discharge are decided by the military authorities. However, if a legitimate claim has been turned down, you can sometimes apply again with new information, or go to a federal court for a writ of habeas corpus, a court order requiring that the armed forces release you. If you believe you were illegally inducted, or that your conscientious objection claim was improperly turned down by Selective Service, you may decide not to refuse induction and face criminal trial and the risk of prison. In that case, immediately after being inducted into the armed forces, you can request a writ of habeas corpus from a federal court. You certainly should not accept induction on the assumption that such action would be successful, since courts seldom grant these requests. You should act only on the advice of a lawyer experienced in this field.

If you are unsuccessful in your application for discharge or for a writ of habeas corpus, you will of course remain in the armed forces. If your conscience forces you to disobey legal orders, you will be subject to court-martial. You are likely to receive a sentence of up to five years in military prison, followed ordinarily by a less-than-honorable discharge.

The Central Committee for Conscientious Objectors can provide information and aid and can refer you to a lawyer (see Chapter 21 for addresses).

PUBLIC HEALTH SERVICE

Other than the civilian work for conscientious objectors discussed in Chapters 14 and 15, there are only two nonmilitary services that fulfill the draft requirements. Both of them are open only to trained professionals.

The Public Health Service provides commissions to doctors, dentists, and other medical specialists, pharmacists, social workers, male nurses, trained therapists, hospital administrators, engineers, scientists, and others whose special skills are related to health. By serving for two years as a commissioned officer doing hospital, research, or public health work, assigned to work either for the Public Health Service (including the National Institutes of Health) or assigned through it to serve the Coast Guard, the Bureau of Prisons, or the Environmental Science Services Administration, you fulfill the requirements of the Selective Service System.

Doctors in the PHS are often assigned to the Coast Guard for six months. No reserve obligations apply to PHS officers, unless they wish to join the PHS Reserve Corps.

While on active duty, commissioned officers in the PHS are classified I-C by their draft boards. After serving the required time, they are classified IV-A.

You can get information by writing to U.S. Public Health Service, Office of Personnel (OSG), 9000 Rockville Pike (NBOC #2), Bethesda, Maryland 20014.

ENVIRONMENTAL
SCIENCE SERVICES ADMINISTRATION

Two years as a commissioned officer in ESSA will also complete the draft obligation, without reserve commitment, but ESSA requires that you enlist for at least three years. This agency is a combination of the Coast and Geodetic Survey, the U.S. Weather Bureau, and the Central Radio Propagation Laboratories of the National Bureau of Standards. Its work involves scientific research and service. You must have at least a bachelor's degree with a major in science or technology to qualify for a commission.

While on active duty, your draft classification is I-C. You receive a IV-A classification when you complete ESSA service.

Information is available from Chief, Commissioned Personnel Branch, Environmental Science Services Administration, Washington Science Center, Rockville, Maryland 20852.

It should be noted that officers of both PHS and ESSA may be transferred to the armed forces in time of war or national emergency, so these are not options for most conscientious objectors. While this is unlikely, if you adopt one of these alternatives you must accept the possibility that it may not keep you from serving in the armed forces.

PART III

DEFERMENT AND EXEMPTION

"While the best known purpose of Selective Service is to procure manpower for the armed forces, a variety of related processes take place outside delivery of manpower to the active armed forces. Many of these may be put under the heading of 'channeling manpower.' Many young men would not have pursued a higher education if there had not been a program of student deferment. Many young scientists, engineers, tool and die makers, and other possessors of scarce skills would not remain in their jobs in the defense effort if it were not for a program of occupational deferments. Even though the salary of a teacher has historically been meager, many young men remain in that job, seeking the reward of a deferment. . . .

"The psychology of granting wide choice under pressure to take action is the American or indirect way of achieving what is done by direction in foreign countries where choice is not permitted. . . .

"Delivery of manpower for induction, the process of providing a few thousand men with transportation to a reception center, is not much of an administrative or financial challenge. It is in dealing with the other millions of registrants that the System is heavily occupied, developing more effective human beings in the national interest."

NATIONAL SELECTIVE SERVICE, "CHANNELING"
(1965)

CHAPTER NINE

STUDENTS: I-S(H), II-S, I-S(C)

Although people often speak of a "student deferment," there isn't just one classification for students. Actually there are five:

1. I-S(H)—high school students
2. II-S—college and some graduate students
3. I-S(C)—college students (and rarely, graduate students) who have received induction orders but are deferred until the end of the academic year
4. II-A—students in non-degree vocational training programs, including trade and business schools, as well as trades apprentices
5. IV-D—most students in seminaries or pre-enrolled in seminaries

The last two are discussed in other chapters—the II-A in Chapter 10, and the IV-D in Chapter 12. The first three are fully discussed in this chapter.

You should keep in mind, however, that this chapter, like the rest of this book, describes the rules as they were at the time the book went to press. The 1967 law and Regulations made a number of changes concerning student deferments, and other important changes have been made since then. Further changes are possible in these controversial rules for student deferments, especially the rules on deferments for graduate study, and therefore these should be watched closely. If you are a student, you should watch the newspapers and stay in touch with your local draft counselor.

I-S(H)

Some draft boards don't classify registrants until they have finished high school. But if yours classifies you while you are still a full-time high-school student, it must give you a I-S(H) deferment until you either reach age 20, leave full-time high school, or graduate [REG 1622.15(a)].

The board will usually believe your statement in Series IX of the Classification Questionnaire (discussed in Chapter 4) that you are a high-school student and give you the I-S(H). But sometimes you may receive a I-A even though you notified the board that you are in high school. In this case, ask your school to give you (or send to the board) a letter saying you are a full-time student there. Send it to the board within 30 days with your own letter asking for a I-S(H) deferment and saying that you want a personal appearance and appeal if the board doubts that you qualify.

The Regulations don't require that your I-S(H) continue after your 20th birthday. Boards in some areas make a policy of not drafting you if you are 20 years old but need additional time to graduate from high school. Others will draft you out of high school if you turn 20. If you need more time to finish high school after you are 20, you should write to your local board explaining how long you will need, asking that the board allow you to finish, and explaining any unusual circumstances. If you are reclassified anyway, the appeal procedures described in Chapter 5 may not get your deferment back but they will give you three to six months to complete your high school education.

If you expect to enter college or vocational school soon after you finish high school, be sure to notify your draft board of these plans. It is a good idea to send the board a copy of your college admission letter and other proof that you will continue your education, such as a copy of your receipt for a tuition deposit.

If you are 18 or younger when you graduate from high school, you are able to take a year off before going to college and remain classified I-A without danger of being drafted, since present rules don't allow drafting anyone younger than 19. This may be especially useful if you need to take some non-credit courses to make up deficiencies and be ready for college, if you need to work for a time to save money for college, or if you need time to mature. Once you enter college, you usually cannot drop out for a time without losing your II-S deferment forever.

II-S

Undergraduate Students

The 1967 draft law, for the first time, requires that all undergraduate college students receive the II-S deferment if they meet the qualifications for it, but it also imposes serious disadvantages for taking it [MSSA 6(h)(1)].

To receive the II-S for undergraduate study, you must meet six requirements [REG 1622.25]:

1. You must request the deferment in writing, either on a Request for Undergraduate Student Deferment (Form 104) or by letter. The form is available from your draft board and from most colleges.

2. You must make sure your college sends a Student Certificate (Form 109 or equivalent) to your draft board, stating that you meet the requirements for the deferment. At most colleges, this is not done automatically; you must ask the school to send it.

APPROVAL NOT REQUIRED.

SELECTIVE SERVICE SYSTEM

REQUEST FOR UNDERGRADUATE STUDENT DEFERMENT

The Military Selective Service Act of 1967 provides in pertinent part as follows:

Section 6. "(h)(1) Except as otherwise provided in this paragraph, the President shall, under such rules and regulations as he may prescribe, provide for the deferment from training and service in the Armed Forces of persons satisfactorily pursuing a full-time course of instruction at a college, university, or similar institution of learning and who request such deferment. A deferment granted to any person under authority of the preceding sentence shall continue until such person completes the requirements for his baccalaureate degree, fails to pursue satisfactorily a full-time course of instruction, or attains the twenty-fourth anniversary of the date of his birth, whichever first occurs. * * * No person who has received a student deferment under the provisions of this paragraph shall thereafter be granted a deferment under this subsection, * * * except for extreme hardship to dependents (under regulations governing hardship deferments), or for graduate study, occupation, or employment necessary to the maintenance of the national health, safety, or interest. * * * Any person who requests and is granted a student deferment under this paragraph, shall, upon the termination of such deferred status or deferment, and if qualified, be liable for induction as a

112

registrant within the prime age group irrespective of his actual age, unless he is otherwise deferred under one of the exceptions specified in the preceding sentence. As used in this subsection, the term 'prime age group' means the age group which has been designated by the President as the age group from which selections for induction into the Armed Forces are first to be made after delinquents and volunteers."

TO: Local Board No. ....

....

....

I have read and understand the preceding provisions of the Military Selective Service Act of 1967. I am pursuing a full-time course of instruction at a college, university, or similar institution of learning, and do hereby request that I be granted an undergraduate student deferment in Class II–S.

....
(Signature)

....
(Number and Street or RFD Route)

....
(Selective Service Number)

....
(City and State)

....
(Date)

....
(ZIP Code)

SSS Form 104 (6-29-67)

U.S. GOVERNMENT PRINTING OFFICE : 1967—O–268-814

113

FORM APPROVED
BUDGET BUREAU NO. 33-R 0124.

SELECTIVE SERVICE SYSTEM

STUDENT CERTIFICATE

(Complete Appropriate Item or Items)

Date _____

Selective Service No.

1. Name and Current Mailing Address of Student

   _____
   (Date)

2. The student identified above has been accepted for admission for a full-time course of instruction at the college, university or similar institution of learning shown below which will commence on or about

   _____
   (Date)

3. The student identified above has entered upon and is satisfactorily pursuing a full-time course of instruction at the college, university, or similar institution of learning shown below in the ☐ 1st ☐ 2nd ☐ 3rd ☐ 4th ☐ 5th year class, which commenced on _____ and is expected to receive a degree on
   (Date)

   or about _____
   (Date)

4. The student identified above completed his ☐ 1st ☐ 2nd ☐ 3rd ☐ 4th year class on _____ at a college, university, or similar institution of learning.
   (Date)

5. The student identified above is (check one) ☐ No longer enrolled
   ☐ Not eligible to continue ☐ Graduated

   _____
   (Date)

114

6. Remarks

INSTRUCTIONS

Selective Service Regulations define a student's academic year as the twelve month period following the **beginning of** his course of study.

This form may be submitted when an individual has been accepted for admission as an undergraduate student in a college, university, or similar institution of learning (Item 2) and will be submitted promptly (1) at the beginning of the student's academic year (Item 3, or Items 3 and 4) or (2) when a student is no longer enrolled, is not eligible to continue, or has graduated (Item 5). When graduation occurs, the date of graduation should be entered in the space following that caption. The original may be forwarded to the State Director of the State in which the institution is located, for distribution to local boards within the State, or to other State Directors of Selective Service, or direct to local boards. When the latter plan is followed the address of the registrant's local board should be in his possession on a Registration Certificate (SSS Form 2 or 2-A) a Notice of Classification (SSS Form 110).

Submission of this form does not constitute a request for deferment.

Authentication of information on this form may be by any means evidencing that a responsible official of the institution has verified its preparation.

7. ADDRESS OF LOCAL BOARD	8. AUTHENTICATION
	_____
	Name and address of Institution

S S S FORM 109 (REVISED 10-11-67)   (PREVIOUS PRINTINGS ARE OBSOLETE)

115

3. You must be receiving credit toward a bachelor's degree for your courses. This means that at some colleges "nonmatriculated" or "special" students may not qualify for II-S deferments, though they may qualify for II-A (see Chapter 10).

4. You must be a full-time student. At many colleges this is defined as twelve or more semester hours, but standards vary from one school to another. Since the law and Regulations don't define "full time," it appears that each college can adopt any definition it considers appropriate.

5. You must be "satisfactorily pursuing a full-time course of instruction." According to the Regulations, this means that you must be completing enough course work each year to receive your degree in the normal number of years. Thus, if you are in a four-year program, you must complete about 25% of your credits by the beginning of your sophomore year, 50% by the beginning of your junior year, and 75% by the beginning of your senior year to continue to receive the deferment. If you are in a five-year program, you must complete about 20% of your credits each year.

6. You must be under 24 years old. If you turn 24, you are likely to lose your II-S deferment, even in the middle of a school year.

Class rank, grades, and test results are no longer used to determine eligibility for II-S.

The Regulations require that you receive the II-S deferment for an entire academic year at a time, unless you graduate or leave full-time study earlier, and your local board should not reclassify before that time [LBM 43]. Since the academic year is defined as "the 12-month period following the beginning of [your] course of study" [REG 1622.25 (b)], you will have the summer to make up any credit you lose in the regular school year.

Your "academic year" doesn't necessarily start in September. If you began the year in September, you will have until the following September. But if you began your year in January or June, your "academic year" must continue until the following January or June.

Some colleges have defined "full time" to give their students the advantages of maximum flexibility in planning their educations. Since the Regulations require that the student take enough courses to be on schedule for graduation, they define "full time" in terms of this requirement: any student taking enough courses to graduate on schedule is considered full-time. Thus the student who has taken extra courses in his early years can take a reduced schedule later and still be full-time if he will graduate on schedule. And a student who takes a reduced schedule but agrees to make it up in summer school, or by taking a heavier schedule later, can be considered full-time if his college feels confident that he will still graduate on schedule. However, only a few colleges have adopted this flexible definition; most still define "full time" in terms of a rigid number of semester hours.

In a few states, the state director of Selective Service has defined "full time" as a stated number of credit hours. Since the Student Certificate form doesn't have a space for the number of semester hours you are taking, this requirement seems unenforceable. In addition, there is no authority in the law or Regulations for the Selective Service System to impose its own definition of "full-time" study. As indicated above, that power seems to belong to the school. It is proper that it should, for educational requirements vary from one college to another, and each should be free to establish standards suitable to its educational plan.

Despite the flexibility available under these rules, there are several ways you can lose your deferment. You may fall behind schedule. If you do, it is likely that most colleges will feel obligated to refuse to provide a Student Certificate (Form 109), or will add a note in the Remarks section indicating that you are not "satisfactorily pursuing" your degree.

Selective Service offers some hope if you have fallen behind schedule. General Hershey has stated that a favorable Student Certificate can be given to a student who has fallen somewhat behind schedule, if his college "is convinced that this deficiency will not delay the expected date of completion of his course of study . . . the intent [of the Regulations] is to indicate that a student should receive his degree in the normal and specified length of time."

The same statement offers hope if you need extra time to graduate. Even if the school won't give you a favorable Student Certificate because you are too far behind to catch up, the local board may use its discretion in giving deferments "when the failure to earn the required credits was due to illness or some other reason which the board considers adequate" (*Selective Service,* September 1967).

The requirement that you complete a certain percentage of your degree credits was added to the 1967 draft law, and it applies only after the date of that law. If you have made normal progress since July 1, 1967, you are eligible for the II-S deferment [LBM 43]. In practice, this is decided by your school, which indicates an estimated graduation date each time it sends in your Student Certificate (Form 109). If you were a college student in the fall of 1967, the probable graduation date your school put on the form then should normally decide how long you will be allowed. If you have earned enough course credits to remain on schedule toward that graduation date, you should be able to keep your II-S (provided, of course, that you meet all the other requirements), regardless of how long you had been in college before July 1, 1967. If you have fallen further behind since then, you may lose your II-S.

In addition, if you have interrupted college to do other things, you may be able to return without having the interruption counted against you if while you were out of school you were classified II-A or IV-D [LBM 83]. Thus you are able to go back to college after time out for Peace Corps or VISTA service (if you receive the usual II-A occupational deferment) or for theological study or missionary work (if you are given the IV-D minister's exemption).

You may also lose your deferment because you are taking fewer courses than your school defines as full-time, or because you start a semester as a full-time student but later find it necessary to drop a course or two. When this happens during a school year, most schools will notify your draft board immediately. They are not obligated to do this. The regulations place the responsibility on you to notify your board of changes, though they encourage others to report information about you [REG 1625.1(b), 1641.7(a)]. But state directors often ask colleges to inform draft boards when students drop out or change from full-time to part-time study, and most schools do so.

The II-S deferment applies equally whether you are a student in a four-year college or in a junior college taking courses which may be applied toward a bachelor's degree. In fact, there may be greater leniency in continuing your deferment if you are behind schedule as a result of junior college credits not being accepted by the senior college [LBM 43]. Only if you are a junior college student in a vocational program, taking courses not transferable to a senior college, are you ineligible for II-S; then you are probably eligible for II-A, discussed in Chapter 10.

As mentioned at the beginning of this section, there are several disadvantages in requesting and receiving an undergraduate II-S student deferment under the 1967 draft law:

1. You can never receive a III-A deferment (discussed in Chapter 11) because of fatherhood [MSSA 6(h)(1), REG 1622.30, LBM 84]. You may still receive the III-A deferment for "extreme hardship to dependents," but it is much harder to get than the fatherhood III-A.

2. Your draft eligibility is extended to age 35. This is true of all deferments, but it has not mattered because in practice you can't be drafted after you reach 26 (for reasons discussed in Chapter 6).

3. You become eligible for a "prime age group" if one is ever formed, and this could actually cause you to be drafted after you are 26 (see page 78 for details).

4. You will not be eligible for a I-S(C) deferment (discussed below) if you get an induction order as a graduate student after you have received your bachelor's degree.

Because of these disadvantages—especially the loss of the fatherhood deferment for married students—many draft counselors advise that you request a II-S deferment only if you don't qualify for any other deferment. You may also be eligible for a I-Y or IV-F for physical conditions, a II-A for essential employment, a IV-A as an only surviving son, a IV-D as a pre-seminary student, a III-A for supporting dependents, or some other classification that will let you continue your education without taking a II-S. Of course, most students aren't eligible for any of these, so they take the II-S and accept its penalties. Any student who has requested and received a II-S since June 30, 1967, has already made himself subject to these four disadvantages, so he may as well continue his II-S as long as he qualifies for it.

However, if you haven't requested and received a II-S deferment since that date, there are several possibilities open to you. If you aren't yet 19 years old, you may avoid requesting a II-S and continue in I-A without danger of being drafted. You should still have your school send the Student Certificate (Form 109) to your draft board, but you shouldn't make written request for the II-S deferment. Even if you are over 19, you may decide to remain I-A if draft calls are low and your local board is drafting only older men. If you decide later that you want a II-S, you must receive it at any time you request it if you still qualify, provided you aren't under an induction order. You may even want to avoid requesting a II-S until you receive an induction order, since a full-time student who receives an induction order during a school term must receive a I-S(C) which cancels the induction order (discussed below). However, if you decide to do this, remember that you may not receive a I-S(C) if the induction order is issued while you are out of school, so you may want to go to summer school or request a II-S if you suspect an induction order may be issued during a vacation period between school terms. You may be especially interested in avoiding a II-S as long as possible if you aren't sure you will remain in college, or if you are married and may become a father.

Graduate and Professional Students

Under present rules, only two groups of graduate and professional students are eligible for II-S deferments.

If you enter graduate study in one of five medical fields—medicine, dentistry, osteopathy, optometry, or veterinary medicine—you must be given a II-S deferment as long as you are "satisfactorily pursuing" your degree, normally until completion of internship [REG 1622.26(a)].

If you are a graduate student in any other field in the fall of 1968 or after, you may be given a II-S deferment at your local board's discretion, provided you meet these very limiting requirements [REG 1622.26(b)]:

1. You must have begun your second year of "post-baccalaureate study" by October 1, 1967. Thus, in the fall of 1968, you probably were at least a third-year student.

2. You must request the deferment by letter (some states provide forms). This isn't required by the Regulations, but by a memorandum from the national director [LBM 84].

3. Your school must send a Graduate or Professional College Student Certificate (Form 103 or equivalent), certifying that you are a full-time student "satisfactorily pursuing" your degree.

4. You must be in "a course of study leading to a doctoral or professional degree or the equivalent (or a combination of master's and doctoral degrees)."

5. You must not have interrupted your graduate study (unless you returned to graduate school in the fall of 1967 after an interruption during all of which you were classified II-A or IV-D [LBM 83]).

The deferment is renewable for a maximum of five years, including time previously spent in graduate study.

The Regulations don't define "satisfactorily pursuing" in the case of graduate students, and the undergraduate definition seems not to apply. Nor is an academic year defined for graduate students.

There is provision in the 1967 law for the National Security

Council to advise Selective Service on occupational and student deferments. The Regulations make it mandatory that II-S deferments be given, not only to medical students, but to graduate students "in such other subjects necessary to the maintenance of the national health, safety, or interest as are identified by the Director of Selective Service upon the advice of the National Security Council."

On February 16, 1968, General Hershey reported that the National Security Council had decided that no fields of graduate study should be designated for deferment, and that he agreed with this decision [LBM 95]. The NSC acted on the advice of the Secretaries of Defense, Labor, Commerce, and Health, Education and Welfare, who were instructed to "maintain a continuing surveillance over the Nation's manpower and educational needs." They could change their minds at any time and designate some, or all, graduate and professional fields for deferment. Unless this is done, or the Regulations are changed, it is probable that a local board lacks the legal power to grant a II-S deferment for graduate study except to the two groups discussed above, though a few boards have given them anyway.

If you request and receive a II-S deferment for graduate study, the Regulations impose the same four penalties as apply to undergraduates. The Selective Service Act imposes loss of the III-A deferment for fatherhood only on those who receive undergraduate deferments [MSSA 6(h)(1)], but the Regulations go farther and apply it to all men who receive II-S deferments after June 30, 1967 [REG 1622.30(a)]; a directive from the national director limits it to those who *requested* and received II-S deferments, so if you are classified II-S without a written request, you are still eligible for the fatherhood III-A deferment [LBM 84] (for further details, see Chapter 11). Whether you are ineligible for a I-S(C) deferment if you have received a II-S for graduate study

☆ U.S. GOVERNMENT PRINTING OFFICE: 1967—279-764

Form Approved
Budget Bureau No. 33-R-0202

SELECTIVE SERVICE SYSTEM

GRADUATE OR PROFESSIONAL COLLEGE STUDENT CERTIFICATE

(Complete Appropriate Item or Items)

Date _____

Selective Service No.

1. Name and Current Mailing Address of Student

PART I – GRADUATE STUDENTS

2 (a). The student identified above has been accepted for admission to graduate school for a full-time course of instruction leading to the degree of _____ in _____ and being the first class commencing _____ in the class commencing _____

2 (b). The student identified above has entered upon a full-time course of instruction as a candidate for a graduate degree, which commenced on _____, and currently is meeting degree requirements, and is expected to attain the degree of _____ in _____, on or about _____.

PART II – PROFESSIONAL STUDENTS

3 (a). The student identified above has been accepted for admission to _____ school in the first year class commencing _____ and being the first class commencing after he completed requirements for admission.

3 (b). The student identified above has entered upon, the _____ year of his professional studies, and is satisfactorily pursuing a full-time course of study leading to graduation with the degree of _____ on or about _____

PART III - GENERAL

4. The student identified above is (check one) ☐ Not eligible to continue ☐ No longer enrolled full time

☐ Graduated

☐ _____ (Date)

5. Remarks

INSTRUCTIONS

Selective Service Regulations define a student's academic year as the twelve month period following the beginning of his course of study.

This form should be submitted when an individual has been accepted for admission as a graduate or a professional student to a college, university, or similar institution of learning (Item 2(a) or 3(a)), and will be submitted promptly (1) at the beginning of a student's academic year (Item 2(b) or 3(b)), or (2) when a student is no longer enrolled, not eligible to continue, or graduated (Item 4). When graduation occurs Item 4 should be completed, entering the date of graduation after that caption.

The original may be forwarded to the State Director of the State in which the institution is located, for distribution to local boards within the State, or to other State Directors of Selective Service, or direct to local boards. When the latter plan is followed the address of the registrant's local board should be in his possession on a Registration Certificate (SSS Form 2 or 2-A) or a Notice of Classification (SSS Form 110). A copy may be furnished to the registrant and a copy returned.

Submission of this form does not constitute a request for deferment.

Authentication of information on this form may be by any means evidencing that a responsible official of the institution has verified its preparation.

6. ADDRESS OF LOCAL BOARD

7. AUTHENTICATION

Name and address of Institution

S S S Form 103 (Revised 10 - 11 - 67) (Previous printings are obsolete)

125

after June 30, 1967, is a subject of controversy; see discussion below.

I-S(C)

The I-S(C) is a curious deferment. It is the only one that you can't get until *after* you've received an induction order. It cancels the induction order and defers you until the end of that academic year, unless you leave school earlier.

Both the Act and the Regulations make it mandatory that a local board give you the I-S(C) deferment on request if you are a full-time student and receive an induction order while you are in school. But there are several important limitations.

First, according to the Regulations, it is available only if you are an undergraduate or one of the few graduate and professional students who either have not received a bachelor's degree or have not received a II-S deferment since June 30, 1967 [REG 1622.15(b), LBM 87].

Second, the I-S(C) classification can be received only once, and it can't be renewed. However, if you had lost your undergraduate II-S because you were behind schedule, then received an induction order and qualified for a I-S(C), it is quite possible that you could use this period to make up enough work to qualify for a II-S again, or you might become eligible for some other classification. After your academic year is over (presumably the same 12-month academic year that applies to the undergraduate II-S deferment, though the Regulations aren't specific), you must be reclassified and have the right to submit new information and have full appeal rights before an induction order can again be issued.

Although the Regulations deny the I-S(C) to all graduate students who have received II-S deferments under the 1967 law and who have bachelor's degrees, the Act seems to deny it only to those who have been given II-S deferments for *undergraduate* study since June 30, 1967 [MSSA 6(h)(1), 6(i)(2)]. Thus, while 1968-69 first-year graduate students who were deferred as undergraduates in 1967-68 would be ineligible for I-S(C), second-year graduate students might be eligible for I-S(C). This discrepancy is unresolved as this book goes to press, but graduate and professional students who receive induction orders during the school year, and who have not been deferred as undergraduates since June 30, 1967, may wish to request I-S(C) deferments and consult draft counselors or attorneys about the status of this dispute. Even if the I-S(C) deferment is denied, National Selective Service has recommended that graduate students who receive induction orders should have them postponed to allow them to finish the current semester or quarter (*Selective Service,* November 1968).

Receiving a I-S(C) deferment has no effect on later III-A deferment as a father, but it will make you eligible for a "prime age group" if one is ever formed.

You will be eligible for a I-S(C) if your induction order is issued during a period when classes are actually in session and you are enrolled in them full-time. (Presumably if you get an induction order between semesters or quarters, or even during registration period but before classes start, you might not get the I-S(C), but this definition seems to have grown up in practice and isn't specified in the Regulations.)

If you receive an induction order while a student, write to your local board requesting a I-S(C) deferment and point out that you were a full-time student on the date the induction order was mailed. Also ask your school to send a new certificate (Form 109 for undergraduates, Form 103 for graduate and professional students), and be sure that two items of information are correctly entered: that you were a full-time student on the date the induction order was issued (this should go into the Remarks section of the form), and the correct date when you began your current academic year so you will receive the I-S(C) until the end of the proper period.

If you are a conscientious objector classified I-O, you do not receive an induction order and are therefore not eligible for I-S(C) deferment. However, if you receive an order to find civilian work (Form 152) or to report for civilian work (Form 153) while you are a full-time student, you are entitled to a postponement until the end of the academic year [paragraph 11 of LBM 64]. This isn't a change of classification, so there are no appeal rights when the academic year is over and the postponement ends. To get the postponement, take the same steps suggested above for getting a I-S(C).

CHAPTER TEN

OCCUPATIONAL, VOCATIONAL TRAINING, AGRICULTURAL, GOVERNMENT OFFICIALS: II-A, II-C, IV-B

In a sense, men who are drafted are selected by a process of elimination. The available manpower pool is so vast that not all can be drafted. Congress therefore decided not to draft those engaged in activities "found to be necessary to the maintenance of the national health, safety, or interest" [MSSA 6(h)(2)], by giving them deferments. Three such deferments are:

1. II-A—any occupation except agriculture, including several types of vocational training

2. II-C—agriculture

3. IV-B—certain elected government officials and judges

The IV-B deferment is provided by Congress for Congressmen and other elected officials at the federal and state levels, and for judges of courts of record. With only 81 men in it as of August 31, 1968, it is easily the most exclusive Selective Service classification.

OCCUPATIONAL DEFERMENT

The II-A and II-C deferments are given for a year or less at a time, but may be renewed as long as you are doing work judged essential by your draft board.

If you work on a farm and want a II-C deferment, or in

some other occupation and want a II-A deferment, you should ask your employer or supervisor to write to your draft board asking that you be deferred. He should emphasize the following points, taken from the Regulations [REG 1622.23(a)]:

1. That the work is "necessary to the maintenance of the national health, safety, or interest." The letter should explain why your product or service is essential to the national economy or defense, or to the community in which you work.

2. That you are actually performing the work, or would be except for a "seasonal or temporary interruption." Merely being trained for an essential occupation isn't enough; you must actually work in it.

3. That without a qualified person in your job, your employer's organization would have "a material loss of effectiveness." This is best shown by describing your job and explaining its contribution to the end product.

4. That another qualified person can't readily be found to take your place, because of a shortage in your field or because you have unique abilities.

In addition to the letter your employer writes, you should write requesting the deferment and making essentially the same points. If your employer doesn't write, your letter alone may sometimes be enough to get you the deferment. But a letter by the employer is usually necessary as well.

An employer who has requested your occupational deferment must be notified of the board's decision. He is sent a Classification Advice (Form 111), illustrated on page 54, at the time you are sent a Notice of Classification (Form 110). He has the same right of appeal as you have, though only you can request a personal appearance. Before appealing, it is usually advisable to have the personal appearance, and if possible to take your employer or supervisor as a witness. If you appeal, you (or your employer) can have the appeal transferred to the state appeal board for the area where you work or live, if different from the one where your local board is, by requesting a transfer in the letter requesting the appeal. This is usually desirable if you are applying for an occupational deferment.

If you are self-employed, of course, you will have to make the request yourself. In that case, you will probably want to get letters from responsible people stating that they know your work and consider it essential, and perhaps to ask one of them to attend your personal appearance.

The comments so far in this chapter apply equally to II-A and II-C deferments. Specific information on each of them follows.

II-A

Typically, draft boards give II-A deferments to highly skilled men in industry, technology, scientific research and development, social service, and teaching. However, there are no longer any official guidelines or job lists for occupational deferment, so your local board can give you a deferment for any kind of job if the board is convinced it is essential. For the same reason, the local board can turn down your request for occupational deferment in one of these fields or any other, even though you and your employer believe the deferment is well justified. It sometimes happens that two employees doing identical work for the same employer, with equal skill and training, apply for occupational deferment to two different draft boards, and one is successful and the other isn't. There is little uniformity among local boards, and all you can do is appeal if your request is rejected.

There are advisory memorandums on several occupations, and if you are in one of these fields you may find it useful to read them and perhaps refer your local board to them: male nurses [LBM 33], doctors and other medical specialists [LBM 77], merchant marine officers [Operations Bulletin 299], skilled workers in the forging and machine tool industries [Operations Bulletin 303]. These can be read and copied at any local board office or state headquarters.

None of these memorandums are binding on your local board. It can do as the national director advises, or ignore his advice. However, not all boards know this, and most boards follow the director's suggestions.

A memorandum issued on April 25, 1968, advises against giving occupational deferments to most graduate-student teaching assistants: "A full-time graduate student shall not be considered for occupational deferment because he is engaged in teaching part time" [LBM 96]. Despite the use of the word "shall," if a local board believes the "national interest" requires giving a II-A deferment to a part-time teaching assistant, or for any other part-time occupation such as research, it has the power to do so. But few are likely to go against the advice of the national director.

In addition, many state directors issue advisory memorandums suggesting policies on occupational deferments. The advice varies widely. For example, one state director may suggest that boards defer experienced, continuing teachers, but hesitate to defer those just out of school and beginning to teach. The director of an adjacent state may suggest deferring all teachers whose schools consider them essential. These memorandums should be available for reading and copying at local boards in that state or at state headquarters. A letter of request to the state headquarters may get you a copy of the state director's current memorandum on your occupation, if he has issued one.

Although there is no uniform policy, most local boards will give you a II-A deferment during service in the Peace Corps, VISTA, and some other government volunteer programs. After this service, you will again be eligible for the draft, unless you qualify for some other deferment. The officials of these programs are generally well informed and helpful in dealing with draft boards.

II-C

Farm workers and owners may qualify for II-C deferment on the same basis as other workers qualify for II-A. However, two additional questions can be considered. First, your local board is supposed to consider whether your farm is at least as productive as others in your area. It will try to determine this by figuring "average annual production per farm worker" for your farm compared with the "local average farm of the type under consideration" [REG 1622.24(b)]. Only production for market is considered, not any used by the farm families.

In addition, under the 1967 Regulations, the board can consider whether there is a surplus or a shortage of the commodities you produce. Presumably it should be more willing to defer you if your products are in short supply, though this isn't required.

Information about computing the productivity of your farm and other aid in trying to get a II-C deferment may be available from your county agricultural agent. He, or the elected stabilization and conservation committee for your county, may also be consulted by the board [LBM 13], so it would be a good idea to see him before you apply.

VOCATIONAL TRAINING

The II-A deferment is given to most men who are receiving vocational training. Unlike the student in college who *must*

Form approved.
Budget Bureau No. 33–R130.

SELECTIVE SERVICE SYSTEM

APPRENTICE DEFERMENT REQUEST

Date _____

1. Name of apprentice	2. Selective Service No.	3. Date of birth
_____		
(Last) (First) (Middle)		(Month) (Day) (Year)

4. Mailing address

_____
(Number and street or R.F.D. route)   (City, town, or village)   (County)   (State)   (ZIP Code)

5. Number and address of local board where registered

6. Name and address of sponsor

7. Name of apprentice training program and activity in which sponsor is engaged

Request is hereby made for the occupational deferment of the person identified in items 1 and 2 of this form as an apprentice in an apprentice training program. The criteria set forth in Selective Service Regulations, as indicated below, have been fulfilled, both as to the individual and the apprentice training program.

8. The apprentice training program identified in item 7 of this form has been accepted for the purpose of deferment by the (check one) ☐ State Director of Selective Service for _____ (State)
☐ Director of Selective Service.

134

9. ☐ The apprentice identified in items 1 and 2 of this form is currently meeting all the standards and requirements of the apprentice training program and is satisfactorily performing and progressing in his on-the-job training and related trade instructions as _____
(Trade or occupation)
apprentice.

Complete item 10 or item 11, whichever is appropriate.

10. ☐ The apprentice identified in items 1 and 2 of this form is engaged in and has completed _____ hours of a term of _____ hours of apprentice training in an activity necessary to the maintenance of the national health, safety, or interest.

11. ☐ The registrant identified in items 1 and 2 of this form is engaged in and has completed _____ hours of a term of _____ hours of apprentice training in an occupation listed as critical on the current list of critical occupations.

12. It is understood that if this deferment request is granted both the registrant and the sponsor are required to notify the local board immediately of any change in the registrant's status as an apprentice. This form must be signed by the registrant, and by the sponsor or his representative.

(Signature of registrant)

(Signature of sponsor or representative)

(Title)

SSS Form 171

135

INSTRUCTIONS

This form is to be prepared by sponsors of accepted apprentice training programs as a request to selective service local boards for the occupational deferment of registrants who are employed as apprentices in such programs and signed by both the registrant and his sponsor. This form is to be completed by filling in all appropriate blank spaces and placing an "X" in each appropriate box. When requested by the registrant a sponsor may submit the original of this form to the registrant's local board at the address shown in item 5. A copy may be furnished to the registrant and a copy may be retained for the sponsor's file.

☆ U.S. GOVERNMENT PRINTING OFFICE : 1965—O—773-961

(Reverse of SSS Form 171)

---

receive a II-S if he meets basic qualifications, you *may* be given a II-A for vocational training at your local board's option.

However, most boards give the II-A deferment to most full-time students in trade, technical, and business schools, to apprentices in recognized and organized apprenticeships, and often to students taking training for other vocations, such as schools for barbers and undertakers. Sometimes these deferments can extend for the period of formal instruction and also a period of required on-the-job training.

Both the national and state directors of Selective Service keep lists of apprentice training programs which they have approved [REG 1622.23(b)(2), 1622.23a(e)], and employers, unions, and others involved in apprenticeship programs know whether they are on them. Only programs on these lists can make you eligible for II-A deferment as an apprentice. The best source of advice is the sponsor of the apprenticeship you are taking or considering taking. Form 171 is used to request deferment of an apprentice.

If you are a student in a technical, trade, business, or other vocational school, you should ask the school to send a letter to your draft board. It should say that you are a full-time student and indicate how long your program will last. In addition, you should write to your board and request the II-A deferment, pointing out that you are a full-time student in a program that does not lead to a college degree [LBM 88].

If you are a junior college student, you will ordinarily be eligible for II-S (see Chapter 9). However, if you are taking a full-time junior-college course which can't be transferred to a senior college and applied toward a bachelor's degree because it is essentially vocational training, you should be eligible for II-A.

Policies vary if you go to college or academic junior college for a time and receive a II-S deferment, then leave to enter a vocational training program. Some state directors suggest that you be given a II-A deferment while you are in vocational school; others suggest that you not be deferred. The decision is up to your local board, though it is likely to follow the state director's advice. If you transfer the other way—out of a vocational program into an academic program leading to a college degree—you should qualify for II-S.

The II-A, like any other deferment, will extend your possible draft age to 35 (though men aged 26 or over are not drafted under present Regulations). However, the II-A does not make you eligible for the "prime age group" or take away your right to III-A deferment as a father. Therefore, if there is a choice, it may be advisable to take a II-A rather than a II-S deferment.

CHAPTER ELEVEN

FATHERS, AND OTHERS WITH DEPENDENTS: III-A

There are actually two types of III-A deferment. If you are a father, you *must* be given a III-A, unless you are disqualified for one of the reasons discussed below. In addition, you *may* be given a III-A because the draft board believes that your dependents will suffer "extreme hardship" if you are drafted. The "fatherhood" III-A is much easier to get if you qualify than the "hardship" III-A because it is usually easy to prove you are a father but usually hard to prove that your dependents will suffer if you can't be with them.

FATHERHOOD III-A

If you send proof (a birth certificate listing you as the father) to your local board that you are a father and that your child lives with you, it must give you the III-A deferment [REG 1622.30(a)]. There are only two exceptions:

1. If you are a doctor, dentist, or other medical specialist, defined by whether you have received the degree in a medical field, whether or not you have completed your training, have received a license to practice, or are practicing your profession, you are not eligible for the fatherhood III-A [REG 1622.30(c)(2)].

2. If you have requested and received a II-S student deferment since June 30, 1967, you are not eligible for the fatherhood III-A.

There seems to be no dispute about the rule on doctors, but there is considerable question about the rule on students. This is because the law only forbids giving you a fatherhood III-A if you have received a II-S deferment as an undergraduate student [MSSA 6(h)(1)]. However, the Regulations go much farther and say that no one who has requested and received a II-S deferment since June 30, 1967, may receive a fatherhood III-A [REG 1622.30(a), LBM 84]. Thus there is dispute about whether you can still be deferred as a father if you have requested and received a II-S since June 30, 1967, solely for graduate study, and probably only a decision in the courts will resolve the question.

If you are not disqualified, the rules for fatherhood III-A are fairly generous. To qualify, you must have "a child or children with whom [you maintain] a bona fide family relationship in [your] home." The Regulation even defines "child":

> The term "child" as used in this section shall include a legitimate or an illegitimate child from the date of its conception, a child legally adopted, a stepchild, a foster child, and a person who is supported in good faith by the registrant in a relationship similar to that of parent and child but shall not include any person 18 years of age or over unless he is physically or mentally handicapped [REG 1622.30(c)(1)].

To qualify for the fatherhood III-A, there is no requirement that you be married, that you be living with your wife, or that you provide any financial support. All that is necessary is that the child live with you.

Nor does the child have to be born yet. Since your child qualifies you for deferment "from the date of its conception," you must be classified III-A as soon as you send your local board a doctor's letter saying (1) that your child has been conceived, (2) the estimated date of birth, and (3) how the pregnancy was diagnosed. In this case, obviously you must be living with your pregnant wife or girlfriend for the child to be living in your home.

However, when an unborn child is the only basis of the III-A deferment, you must send the board the doctor's letter before an induction order is issued or you may not receive the deferment [REG 1622.30(c)(3)]. Despite this Regulation, it may be possible to show that you didn't learn of the pregnancy until after the induction order was issued. If so, learning that the child is expected is "a change in the registrant's status resulting from circumstances over which the registrant had no control" [REG 1625.2], and the local board may reopen the classification and cancel the induction order. Again, the question is in dispute. If you learn only after you receive an induction order that you are to be a father, you should immediately seek the assistance of a very experienced draft counselor or attorney.

You may lose your III-A deferment if you are divorced or separated from your wife and the child is in her custody. However, if the child spends part of the time with you, and if you regularly provide for the child in your home, it is possible that you may still qualify. Even if you can't qualify for the fatherhood III-A, your contributions to the child's support may make you eligible for the "hardship" III-A, discussed below.

Your draft board may question your eligibility for the fatherhood III-A if you aren't married. It may be helpful to send the board a copy of the child's birth certificate bearing your name as father. If the child isn't your own but you are caring for him in your home, you may need to send the board letters by neighbors, a minister, a social worker, or others who can testify that the child does in fact live in your home and is dependent upon you.

If you are caring for younger brothers or sisters because your parents are dead or missing, you should be eligible for a fatherhood III-A for a "relationship similar to that of parent and child," and you will need to get letters testifying to the relationship. If you are caring for a handicapped person older than 18, you will probably need a doctor's letter about the handicap as well as evidence that you care for him as a parent would.

HARDSHIP III-A

A local board will give you a III-A deferment if it is convinced that there is no way to prevent "extreme hardship" to your dependents except by deferring you. You do not lose your right to a hardship III-A because you are a doctor or received a student deferment, and it isn't necessary for the dependent to live with you, so many men who don't qualify for the fatherhood III-A can get a hardship III-A.

This deferment can be given to prevent hardship

> ... (1) to [your] wife, divorced wife, child, parent, grandparent, brother, or sister ... or (2) to a person under 18 years of age or a person of any age who is physically or mentally handicapped ....

However, the dependent must be a U.S. citizen or live in the U.S. or its possessions [REG 1622.30(b)].

The test is whether the dependent needs you. The need may be some form of the following:

1. Financial—you may be deferred if your contributions are essential to the dependent's income and won't be replaced by Army pay and allowances or relatives if you are drafted.

2. Psychological—whether or not you provide financial support, you may be deferred if the dependent would

have an emotional breakdown or severe psychological troubles if you were drafted; you will need to send your draft board letters by a psychiatrist, psychologist, family doctor, or other expert saying so.

3. Personal services—whether or not you provide financial support, you may be deferred if the dependent needs your assistance in managing the day-to-day affairs of the home, providing nursing or therapy, or other services, and no one else can reasonably be expected to take your place.

If you claim that "extreme hardship" to your dependents would result from drafting you, your local board is likely to try to determine whether your support can be replaced. If your dependent is getting welfare payments in addition to your aid, the board may ask the welfare agency whether it would increase the welfare if you were drafted (the answer is likely to be yes). If your dependent is not a child, the board is likely to want to know whether he can support himself. If you are supporting a parent or some other person who is old or disabled, you should get doctors' letters and other evidence to show that he can't work or at least can't earn enough to support himself.

The board will usually send a Dependency Questionnaire (Form 118) if you claim a hardship III-A (see form starting on page 144), and it will use your answers to Series III to try to decide whether another relative would (not just *could,* but *would*) take over the support. If there are relatives but they can't or won't contribute enough to replace your support, you should get letters from them or others who know your family situation (a clergyman's letter is often helpful) explaining why they can't help.

In Series I, Question 3, of the Dependency Questionnaire,

enter the total income of each dependent from all sources in the box marked "Approximate Annual Income." Include not only cash income but such things as the rent on his home even if paid by you (if five people live in the apartment, the dependent's share is one-fifth of the rent or mortgage payment). In the last column, marked "Amount Contributed by Me Annually," enter the contribution you make to this dependent's income, including not only cash but the value of anything else you provide—a share of the rent, food, clothing, medical and other bills you pay, health or other insurance you pay for. You aren't required to contribute any particular portion of the dependent's income. You must show that your support is necessary, that removing it would leave the dependent in "extreme hardship."

The board will also consider whether the Army will pay a dependency allowance. These allowances are paid to some dependents of servicemen. The armed forces will count your wife, unmarried legitimate children under 21, and unmarried stepchildren and adopted children under 21 who are dependent on you. In addition, if they were receiving more than half of their support from you, they will count parents, stepparents and adopted parents, people who have had a relationship to you like that of parents, and permanently disabled legitimate children over 21. No other relatives or other dependents can receive this allowance. If you have dependents who qualify, the armed forces will deduct $40 a month from your pay and add an additional amount depending on how many qualified dependents you have. The total amount payable to the dependent is $95.20 a month for one dependent, $123.10 for two, or $145 for three or more [LBM 17]. To qualify for the III-A hardship deferment on financial grounds, you would have to show that your dependents wouldn't qualify for the allowance or that it

Form approved
Budget Bureau No. 33-R158.5.

SELECTIVE SERVICE SYSTEM

DEPENDENCY QUESTIONNAIRE

DATE QUESTIONNAIRE RETURNED

Date of Mailing ....

COMPLETE AND RETURN BEFORE ....

(Local Board Stamp)

1. Name of Registrant	2. Selective Service No.	3. Date of Birth	4. Class
(Last) (First) (Middle)		(Month) (Day)	
5. Mailing address			
(Number and street or R.F.D. route)			
(City, town, or village) (County) (State) (Zip code)			

(The above items, except the date questionnaire returned, are to be filled in by the local board clerk before questionnaire is mailed)

INSTRUCTIONS

The law requires you to complete and return this questionnaire on or before the date shown to the right above in order that your local board will have information to enable it to classify you. When the questions in any series do not apply, enter "NONE" or "DOES NOT APPLY." Enter on page 4 any additional information which you believe pertinent. Your claimed dependent may also enter on page 4 such additional information as he or she desires.
FILL OUT WITH TYPEWRITER, OR PRINT IN INK, EXCEPT SIGNATURES.

(Member, Executive Secretary or Clerk of Local Board)

144

STATEMENTS OF THE REGISTRANT

CONFIDENTIAL AS PRESCRIBED IN THE SELECTIVE SERVICE REGULATIONS

Series I.—MARITAL STATUS AND DEPENDENTS

1. (a) I (check one): ☐ have never been married   ☐ am a widower
    ☐ am married   ☐ am divorced

    (b) I (check one if applicable): ☐ DO ☐ DO NOT live with my wife; if not, her address is ....

    ....

    (c) We were married at ...., on ....
    (Place)   (Date)

2. (a) I have the following children under 18 years of age who live with me in my home:

    Name.. Age................ Name................ Age................

    Name................ Age................ Name................ Age................

    (b) If you have no child other than an unborn child, attach a statement from a physician showing the basis for his diagnosis of pregnancy and the expected date of birth.

3. The following persons, other than children listed in 2(a) above, are wholly or partially dependent upon me for support. I contribute the amounts, and they have, to my knowledge, income as shown. If income is shown, indicate in Series VII on page 4.— (a) name of employer and, (b) nature of employment. If income is from other than wages or salary, describe sources. If any dependent is physically or mentally handicapped, a physician's statement as to the condition should be attached.

Dependent	Relationship	Age	Approximate Annual Income	Amount Contributed By Me Annually
Name			$	$
Address				
Name			$	$
Address				
Name			$	$
Address				
Name			$	$
Address				

SSS Form 118   (Revised 10–30–64)   (Previous printings may be used)

(1)

145

SERIES II—PERSONS WITH WHOM DEPENDENTS ARE LIVING

When a claimed dependent listed in Series I, Item 3, is living in a household other than the registrant's, or his own, fill in this series.

Name of Dependent	Name of and Relationship of Person With Whom the Dependent Lives

SERIES III—REGISTRANT'S FAMILY

List below all the living members of your immediate family who are 16 years of age or over (except those shown in Series I) including your father, mother, brothers, sisters, father-in-law and mother-in-law. (Use page 4 if necessary.)

	RELATIONSHIP	AGE	CAN THIS RELATIVE CONTRIBUTE TO SUPPORT OF CLAIMED DEPENDENTS [1]
Name Address			☐ YES ☐ NO
Name Address			☐ YES ☐ NO
Name Address			☐ YES ☐ NO
Name Address			☐ YES ☐ NO
Name Address			☐ YES ☐ NO
Name Address			☐ YES ☐ NO

f I like to contribute in detail on page 4.

146

SERIES IV—EMPLOYMENT STATUS OF REGISTRANT

1. My total income from all sources during the last 12 months was $ .... Of this amount, $ ....
   was in salary or wages, $ .... was in other income.

2. The job I am now working at is .... (Give full title of your job)

3. I do the following kind of work .... (State exactly what you do)

4. My average earnings from this employment are $ .... per week, before taxes.

5. My employer is ....
   (Name of company or proprietor. If working for yourself, enter "Self")
   ....
   (Address of place of employment—Street or rural route, city, and State)

   I have worked at this job since .... , 19..........

6. I have been unemployed since .... , 19..........

7. I speak fluently the following foreign languages or dialects ....

8. I read and write well the following foreign languages or dialects ....

SERIES V—FINANCIAL CONDITION

1. I (Check one) ☐ DO ☐ DO NOT own my own home. Monthly payments are $ ....

2. The amount of the original mortgage was $ .... Balance now due $ ....

3. I pay rent in the amount of $ .... per month to ....
   (Name and address of landlord)

4. I have other monthly obligations in the amount of $ .... for ....

5. I (Check one) ☐ DO ☐ DO NOT own an automobile, used primarily for ....

(2)

147

SERIES VI—EMPLOYMENT STATUS OF REGISTRANT'S WIFE

1. My wife (Check one) ☐ IS ☐ IS NOT working at a job for pay.

2. She is employed by ....

   .... (Employer)

   as ....
   (Position or kind of work)

3. Her earnings are $ .... per ☐ HOUR ☐ DAY ☐ MONTH ☐ YEAR

4. She was last employed on ....
   (Date employment ended—if never employed, so state)

   by ....
   (Name of wife's former employer)

REGISTRANT'S CERTIFICATE

I certify that I am the registrant named and described in the foregoing statements in this questionnaire; that I have read (or have had read to me) the statements made by and about me and that each and every such statement is true and complete to the best of my knowledge, information, and belief.

Registrant sign here ☞

....
(Signature or mark of registrant)

Date ....

....
(No. and Street or P.O. address)

148

(City)   (State)   (Zip Code)

Telephone No. --

(Signature of witness to mark of registrant)

If another person has assisted you in completing this questionnaire, such person shall sign the following statement:

I have assisted the registrant herein named in preparation of this questionnaire because --

----
(For example—registrant unable to read and write English, etc.)

(Signature of person who has assisted)

(No. and Street or P.O. address)

(City)   (State)   (Zip Code)

Date --

NOTICE TO REGISTRANT

YOU OR YOUR DEPENDENT MAY ENTER ON PAGE 4 ANY ADDITIONAL STATEMENT WHICH YOU BELIEVE SHOULD BE BROUGHT TO THE ATTENTION OF THE LOCAL BOARD IN DETERMINING YOUR CLASSIFICATION.

(3)

SERIES VII—STATEMENT OF REGISTRANT

(Use additional sheets if necessary)

(Signature of registrant)

(Date)

SERIES VIII—STATEMENT OF DEPENDENT
(Use additional sheets if necessary)

- - - - - - - - - - -

_____
(Signature of dependent)

_____
(Date)

(4)

U.S. GOVERNMENT PRINTING OFFICE : 1968 OF—298-538

151

wouldn't be enough to replace your support and prevent "extreme hardship." In fact, it is extremely difficult to get a III-A on purely financial grounds.

Of course, no amount of money can replace you if the dependency is based on psychological problems or your personal services, and the law recognizes this [MSSA 6(h)(2), REG 1622.30(d)]. When these kinds of dependency exist in addition to or instead of the financial dependency, you should emphasize this in letters to your draft board and get others to write testifying that they know your dependents would have great difficulty in getting along without you.

Letters in support of an "extreme hardship" claim can best be written by your family friends, neighbors, family doctor, psychiatrist, minister, employer, social worker, and others who know the family situation.

A most useful letter will often be written by the dependent himself, if able to do so. In addition to your own letter and form, and the letters you get from other people, you should ask your dependent to write to your local board explaining the situation and asking that you be deferred. When this is done, the dependent must be notified of the draft board's decision when you are, and has the same right to appeal as you have.

However, only you have the right to ask for a personal appearance with your local board, and you should use this opportunity if you possibly can. When your personal appearance is scheduled, you should take your best witness with you. That will often be the dependent himself, even if a child, but sometimes you will be wiser to take your minister or doctor or some other person who can explain the situation to the board. You should also take copies of financial records to prove your support, including canceled checks or receipts for rent and medical or other bills, and income tax returns for you and your dependents.

The III-A deferment for extreme hardship to dependents is one of the hardest classifications to get. The Dependency Questionnaire may be confusing, it may be hard to get enough evidence, and it will often be hard to convince the board that the hardship is real.

This deferment should be available to men from really poor families who are trying to help out, but in practice they often are unable to get it because they don't have records or don't write or speak well enough to explain the situation to a draft board. As a result, this deferment is given mainly to middle-class men because they are more articulate and can convince the board. The help of a draft counselor is especially important when you are applying for this deferment. He may be able to explain the form, help you get evidence, and help you find people who can testify for you.

CHAPTER TWELVE

MINISTERS,
MEN PREPARING FOR THE MINISTRY: IV-D
ALIENS: IV-C
VETERANS, SOLE SURVIVING SONS: IV-A

This chapter discusses three unrelated classifications. If you are eligible for one of these you will probably receive it without difficulty when you send your draft board the necessary evidence. However, a relatively small number of men who claim one of these classifications run into difficulties, and these few have very complicated draft problems. If you are one of these, the brief discussion in this chapter will be inadequate. You will need the help of an expert counselor, one of the national draft counseling services listed in Chapter 21, or possibly an attorney experienced in dealing with these problems.

MINISTERS, SEMINARY STUDENTS,
AND PRE-SEMINARY STUDENTS

By act of Congress, the IV-D classification must be given to you if you are in one of the three groups that qualify for this exemption [MSSA 6(g), REG 1622.43] :

1. "Regular or duly ordained ministers of religion."

2. Full-time seminary students sponsored by denominational bodies.

3. Full-time students preparing to enter seminaries in which they are pre-enrolled, who are sponsored by denominational bodies.

The law defines the two types of ministers who must be

given the IV-D classification [MSSA 16(g)]. You are a "duly ordained" minister if you have received the ordination ritual of a church or sect, and preach and teach the principles of your religion as your "regular and customary vocation." You are a "regular" minister if you are not ordained but preach and teach the principles of your religion as your "customary vocation" and are recognized by your religion as a minister. In either case, you must be qualified to conduct the "public worship" of your faith, and must serve a body of believers or potential believers. The definition in the law, as interpreted by the courts in many complicated cases, should be broad enough to include ministers of unconventional religions, including those who preach in public places and from door to door, provided they meet the "customary vocation" requirement.

You may fulfill the "customary vocation" part of the definition if your ministerial duties are your principal activity, receiving the greatest part of your working time and attention. The complications arise when you work part of the time as a minister and part of the time at an unrelated job, and many court decisions have tried to deal with this situation. Some courts have ruled that you can receive the IV-D classification if you give more hours per week to ministerial duties than to other work, and Selective Service traditionally considers 100 hours per month the minimum time you must spend on ministerial duties to qualify. But these are only general guidelines and some exceptions have been made. The general principle seems to be that the IV-D registrant must give first place in his life to his duties as a minister, and regard his other work merely as a means to continue his religious service.

You may be in the second group entitled to the IV-D classification if you are a full-time student in a "recognized" theological or divinity school under the direction of a "recognized" church or religious organization. To be "recognized," a theological school "should enjoy a good reputation and its graduates should be accepted, by the church sponsoring the registrant, for ministerial duties." A "recognized" church or religious organization "should be able to show that it was established on the basis of a community of faith and belief, doctrines and practices of a religious character, and that it engages primarily in religious activities" [LBM 56]. The local board is required to decide whether the school and church are "recognized," but may ask the advice of state and national directors of Selective Service. There are no official lists, nor could there be without a probable violation of the First Amendment to the Constitution.

If you are applying for a IV-D classification as a seminary student, you will need to send your local board a statement from your sponsoring church or organization saying that you are preparing for the ministry under its direction. You should also have your school send a statement showing that you are "satisfactorily pursuing a full-time course of instruction."

You may be in the third group of IV-D registrants if you are pre-enrolled in a "recognized" seminary under the direction of a "recognized" church or religious organization and you are a full-time, satisfactory student in a course of instruction which will prepare you for admission to the seminary. Thus if you are a college student preparing for a ministerial career, you may avoid receiving a II-S deferment. If you qualify as a pre-enrolled, sponsored preparatory student, you may be classified IV-D. You would need to submit the same kind of evidence as the seminary student.

ALIENS

Relatively few aliens are eligible for the IV-C classification. Many noncitizens are exempted from even registering for the

American draft (see page 26). Most aliens admitted for permanent residence (immigrants) are subject to the draft just as citizens are, except when they are outside the United States. There are special provisions for those admitted as temporary residents (nonimmigrants).

If you are a permanent resident alien, you must register for the draft and are subject to the same rules as registrants who are U.S. citizens. There are two exceptions. By ruling of the U. S. Attorney General, if you are a citizen of one of the 15 countries (listed on page 26) which have treaties providing for exemption of their citizens while they are in the U.S., you may be classified IV-C even though you are a permanent resident of the U.S. if you file an Application by Alien for Relief from Training and Service in the Armed Forces (Form 130), but filing this form will permanently bar you from U.S. citizenship.

In addition, if you are an alien with status as a permanent resident of the U.S., you are classified IV-C during any period when you are outside the United States and its territories. This reclassification would have the effect of canceling an induction order if one had been issued to you, but would not cancel your delinquency status if you had already violated the Selective Service law before leaving the country [REG 1622.42(c)]. If you are an alien and plan to travel outside the United States but want to be able to return, you should notify your local board by letter before you leave, or within 10 days after you leave, of your address abroad, the intended date of return, and the reasons for your trip, enclosing evidence if possible of the reasons for traveling abroad. This can be important because you may be denied readmission to the U.S. or later deported if you have left to avoid military service, so evidence that your trip was necessary because of a family emergency, business, education, or other legitimate purpose may help insure that you can return. Before you

Form approved.
Budget Bureau No. 21-R114.2.

SELECTIVE SERVICE SYSTEM

APPLICATION BY ALIEN FOR RELIEF FROM TRAINING AND SERVICE IN THE ARMED FORCES

_____, 19____
(Date)

(LOCAL BOARD STAMP)

STATE OF _____
} ss:
COUNTY OF _____

I, _____ _____ _____
(Last name)   (First name)   (Middle name)

do solemnly swear (or affirm) that I am a citizen of _____ ; I am a
(Country)

registrant of Local Board _____ , _____ , _____ ;
(Number)   (City)   (County)   (State)

my Selective Service number is [☐ ☐ ☐] ; my alien registration number is _____ ;

I last entered the United States on _____ at _____
(Month, day, and year)   (Place of entry)

on _____ as _____
(Name of vessel)   (Specify visitor, student, crew member, stowaway, or other)

for the purpose of _____ under a
(Study, travel, etc.)

_____ Visa numbered _____ and that I have not been
(Type of visa)   (Number of visa)

admitted to the United States for permanent residence.

I hereby apply for relief from liability for training and service in the Armed Forces of the United States. I have read the NOTICE given below, and I understand that I will forever lose my right to become a citizen of the United States, and I may also be prohibited from entry into the United States or its territories or possessions as a result of filing this application.

Subscribed and sworn to before me this ....

day of ...., 19 ....

....
(Signature of registrant)

....
(Signature of person administering oath)

....
(Title of person administering oath)

NOTICE

Section 4 (a) of Title I of the Universal Military Training and Service Act, as amended, provides in part that "Any male alien who is between the ages of 18 years and 6 months and 26 years, at the time fixed for registration, or who attains the age of 18 years and 6 months after having been required to register pursuant to section 3 of this title, or who is otherwise liable as provided in section 6 (h) of this title, who has remained in the United States in a status other than that of a permanent resident for a period exceeding 1 year (other than an alien exempted from registration under this title and regulations prescribed thereunder) shall be liable for training and service in the Armed Forces of the United States, except that any such alien shall be relieved from liability for training and service under this title if, prior to his induction into the Armed Forces he has made application to be relieved from such liability in the manner prescribed by and in accordance with rules and regulations prescribed by the President; but any alien who makes such application *shall thereafter be debarred from becoming a citizen of the United States.*" (Italics supplied.) Under other existing law, an alien at the time of execution of this application not being a permanent lawful resident of the United States, thereafter becomes barred from ever making an entry for permanent residence into the United States, including Alaska, Hawaii, Puerto Rico, and the Virgin Islands unless he enters as a minister of any religious denomination or as a professor of a college, academy, seminary, or university.

(OVER)

SSS Form No. 130 (Revised 9-1-51)   16—64422-2

159

INSTRUCTIONS

This form shall be executed by the registrant in duplicate. The local board shall forward the original to the Director of Selective Service through the State Director of Selective Service and shall retain the duplicate in the registrant's Cover Sheet (SSS Form No. 101).

The oath may be administered by—

(1) Any civil officer authorized to administer oaths generally.

(2) Any commissioned officer of the land or naval forces assigned for duty with the Selective Service System.

(3) Any member or clerk of a local board or board of appeal.

(4) Any Government Appeal Agent or Associate Government Appeal Agent.

(5) Any duly authorized Advisor to Registrants.

(6) Any postmaster, acting postmaster, or assistant postmaster.

U. S. GOVERNMENT PRINTING OFFICE   16—60450-1

leave, you should also apply for a Permit for Registrant to Depart from the United States (Form 300); even if it is denied, applying for it would help to show your intention to return (for details, see Chapter 7). When you return to the United States, you should write to your local board within 10 days that you are back, and it must then reclassify you, giving you full appeal rights.

If you are a temporary resident alien but are required to register, you must be classified IV-C until your time in the U.S. totals more than one year, whether in one visit or several added together [REG 1622.42(a)].

After you have been in the country as a temporary resident for over a year, you are taken out of the IV-C classification, but are eligible for any other classification a citizen could qualify for. However, even after a year's residence, you may receive the IV-C classification by filing an Application by Alien for Relief from Training and Service in the Armed Forces (Form 130) at any time before you are actually inducted into the armed forces [MSSA 4(a), REG 1622.42(b), LBM 23]. Filing this form with your local board will permanently bar you from U.S. citizenship. It may also make it difficult to get readmitted to the U.S. if you leave, so if you plan to travel outside the U.S. after filing the Form 130 but want to return, you should get the advice of an attorney experienced in immigration law before you leave.

If you registered at a time when you were required to, but have since become a member of one of the groups exempted from registration (discussed on page 26) you should be classified IV-C when you notify your local board of the changed circumstances [REG 1622.42(d)]. This may apply if you are a temporary resident and become an employee of the embassy or United Nations mission of your country, for example, or if you are a temporary or permanent resident and are living in the Canal Zone. It should also apply if you are a physician or other medical specialist in the United States for training or research, were admitted as an immigrant before July 1, 1967, after you were 26 years old, and leave the United States before you are ordered inducted into military service and are readmitted as a J-1 nonimmigrant [LBM 23]. It may also apply if you were a U.S. citizen but emigrated to another country and renounced your U.S. citizenship before the date you were scheduled for induction into the armed forces (see Chapter 17 for discussion of this complex subject).

You are also eligible for the IV-C classification as a temporary U.S. resident during any period when you are outside the country, but may have even more difficulty being readmitted than a permanent resident would (see discussion above).

In addition, whether you are a temporary or permanent U.S. resident, if you have served at least 18 months in the armed forces of a country with which the U.S. has a mutual defense treaty, you may be eligible for the IV-A classification (see discussion below).

VETERANS AND SOLE SURVIVING SONS

If you have completed military service in the U.S. armed forces, you may be classified IV-A, depending on how long you have served and the type of discharge you received. You must receive the IV-A classification:

1. If you were discharged or transferred to the reserves *for the convenience of the government* after serving honorably on active duty in any branch of the armed forces for at least six months [REG 1622.40(a)(1)]. This does not include active duty for training for reservists.

2. If you have served honorably on active duty in any

branch of the armed forces for at least one year [REG 1622.40(a)(2)].

3. If you have served as a commissioned officer in the Public Health Service or the Environmental Science Services Administration for at least two years [REG 1622.40(a)(3)] (for information about this type of service, see Chapter 8).

4. If you have completed the full enlistment term as a member of the Ready Reserves of any branch of the armed forces, or as a member of a National Guard unit (usually six to eight years) [REG 1622.40(a)(5), (6), (7), (8), (9)].

Two other groups of registrants are eligible for the IV-A classification.

If you have performed at least 18 months of active duty in the armed forces of another country, you may receive the IV-A classification, provided that the other country has a mutual defense agreement with the United States and that it exempts from its armed forces American citizens who have served for 18 months in the U.S. armed forces [REG 1622.40(a)(4)]. There are 44 countries with such agreements [listed in LBM 76]. If you qualify for this exemption, you should ask the embassy or a consulate of the country in whose armed forces you have served to send your local board a certificate written in English verifying your service.

If you are the only living son in your family, and either your father or a brother or sister died as a result of service in the U.S. armed forces, whether on active duty or as a result of injury or disease received in military service, you must be classified IV-A as a sole surviving son [MSSA 6(o), REG 1622.40(a)(10)]. You may be eligible for this exemption even if your father is still living, for example if your only brother died as a result of military service. If you are entitled to this classification, you should send your local board a copy of a document showing that a member of your family died as a result of service in the armed forces; if you don't have evidence, the Veterans Administration may be able to help you get it. Draft boards can usually get this sort of information from the Veterans Administration, and it may be useful to ask your local board to write directly to the VA.

CHAPTER THIRTEEN

REJECTION FOR PHYSICAL, MENTAL, OR ADMINISTRATIVE REASONS: I-Y, IV-F

You are found fit or unfit for military service according to standards set up by the Army, not by the Selective Service System. The same standards should apply whether you are being considered for regular military service, noncombatant military service, or civilian work as a conscientious objector. There are no differences between the physical standards for men who enlist and men who are drafted (with the exception of doctors and other medical specialists), and the same physical standards apply to all branches of military service, but there may be different mental (intelligence) standards. Different standards may also apply to those who want special assignments within a branch of the service, such as submarine duty in the Navy or pilot training in the Air Force.

The physical and psychological standards are in Chapter 2 (Medical Fitness Standards for Appointment, Enlistment, and Induction) of Army Regulation 40-501. This chapter (and additional sections in appendices) consists of a list of medical and other conditions which will disqualify you for military service. The list is too long to include in this book, but you can get a complete copy of the regulation for $1.50 from the Superintendent of Documents, Government Printing Office, Washington, D.C. 20402. Order catalog item D 101.9–AR 40-501 Reprint, *Medical Service: Standards of Medical Fitness* (including Changes 1-22).

If you have a condition listed in Chapter 2 of this

regulation, you cannot serve in the armed forces except in case of war or national emergency, and you should be classified I-Y. If your condition is also listed in Chapter 6 (Medical Fitness Standards for Mobilization), you are not acceptable even in wartime and you should be classified IV-F.

If you have a disqualifying condition, you can be reclassified I-Y or IV-F on the basis of an evaluation by your local board, usually based on the recommendation of its medical advisor, or more often at a pre-induction physical examination, or at an examination when you are sent for induction. This chapter discusses these procedures and suggests ways to be sure any disqualifying condition you have is properly recognized.

INTERVIEW WITH LOCAL BOARD MEDICAL ADVISOR

You are required to notify your local board in writing within 10 days after you learn of any change in your circumstances which could affect your classification [REG 1641.7(a)]. This includes information about your physical and mental condition, and information about criminal convictions which could affect administrative (sometimes called "moral") acceptability.

If you are classified I-A, I-A-O, or I-O and you notify your local board that you have one of the medical conditions on the official list [AR 40-501, Chapter 2], the local board must order you to have an interview with its medical advisor (see page 21) to determine whether you should be reclassified [REG 1628.2(b)]. Many local boards seem not to know about this requirement in the Regulations, so you should specifically request an interview with the medical advisor; it may even be useful to call the board's attention to Regulation 1628.2(b) in your letter.

This interview can be transferred if you are so far from

your local board that traveling to see its medical advisor would be a hardship. When you receive the Notice to Registrant to Appear for Medical Interview (Form 219), you should take it to a nearby local board and arrange for transfer in the same way as for an armed forces physical examination (see page 74).

The medical advisor, who serves without pay, can consider any evidence you have submitted to him or to the local board [REG 1628.3], so you should submit all the evidence you can get from your own doctors, hospitals, or other sources. There is little point in asking for a medical interview for a minor condition not on the list.

You should ask your own doctors to write (and preferably type) full reports of your disqualifying condition, including a complete description in medical terms, the medical history, the ways in which the condition may disable you under military conditions, any treatment you need or are receiving, and how long the condition is likely to last. The reports should include copies of X-rays, laboratory reports, special tests, or other evidence of the existence or seriousness of the condition. If medical consultants were involved in diagnosing it, their reports should also be included. If you had to be hospitalized or had an operation, including a copy of the hospital record may be useful.

All evidence given to you should be photocopied so you will have at least four extra copies made for your personal file. Send the originals to your local board when you request the interview with the medical advisor. Take another copy to the medical advisor when he interviews you. These items won't be returned to you; they will be kept by your local board and become a part of your official file.

At the interview, the medical advisor can perform whatever examination he considers necessary, but he cannot have X-rays or laboratory tests made. He then sends his report to

Approval
Not Required.

SELECTIVE SERVICE SYSTEM

NOTICE TO REGISTRANT TO APPEAR FOR MEDICAL INTERVIEW

(Local Board Stamp)

Date of mailing

| (Month) | (Day) | (Year) |

Selective Service No.

You are hereby directed to report for a medical interview at the place and time designated below:

on _____ at _____
    (Date)   (Hour)

_____
(Place of reporting)

(Member, Executive Secretary, or clerk of Local Board)

IMPORTANT NOTICE

This medical interview will be of a preliminary nature, for the purpose of disclosing those obvious defects or manifest conditions which would disqualify you for service in the armed forces, and will not finally determine your acceptability for military service. Should you be found to have no obviously disqualifying defects you will be ordered to report for an Armed Forces Physical Examination.

If you are so far from the place designated above that reporting in compliance with this Notice will be a hardship, take this Notice immediately to the local board for the area in which you are now located and make written request for a transfer for medical interview.

Failure to comply with this Notice will result in your being declared a delinquent and subject to the penalties provided by the Military Selective Service Act of 1967.

SSS FORM   219   (Revised 2-6-64)   (Previous printings may be used)

GPO 941-633

169

the local board. If he considers you unsuitable for military service, the local board can reclassify you I-Y or IV-F, though it isn't required to. During the 1967 fiscal year, nearly 125,000 men were found disqualified by local boards without armed forces physical examinations.

If you are not deferred as a result of the interview with the the medical advisor, you must still receive the armed forces physical examination before you can be inducted. Thus, the medical interview is an extra process which may be helpful in getting your disqualifying condition properly considered or may do you no good, but it can't take away any of your rights. Of course, the medical advisor's opinion may influence the doctors at the later examination.

The interview with the medical advisor is intended as a way to screen men whose conditions can be recognized without the expense and paperwork involved in an armed forces physical examination [LBM 78]. It therefore is improper for a local board to send you for a regular pre-induction examination at the Armed Forces Examining and Entrance Station in place of the medical interview, although this is sometimes done.

The interview with the medical advisor can also be useful if you have already taken and passed a pre-induction physical examination and later discover that you have a disqualifying condition, but in this situation Selective Service takes the view that the re-evaluation should be made by the Examining and Entrance Station, not the medical advisor, despite the apparent conflict with the Regulations (Operations Bulletin No. 327, issued by the director of Selective Service on August 23, 1968).

PRE-INDUCTION PHYSICAL EXAMINATION

The pre-induction physical examination (also called armed

forces physical examination) must be taken and passed before you can be ordered for induction into the armed forces (see Chapter 6 for detailed discussion), unless you are a draft delinquent or a volunteer for induction. Even delinquents and volunteers are sometimes sent for the examination before they are ordered to report for induction; the decision is up to each local board.

After it orders you to take a pre-induction physical examination, your local board should send all evidence in your file that relates to your medical condition to the Armed Forces Examining and Entrance Station (AFEES), including any evidence previously considered by the local board medical advisor. However, to guard against the possibility that some evidence may not reach the AFEES, you should take one of your own copies of the evidence of your disqualifying condition with you to the examination. If you didn't send evidence to your local board, or if the evidence in your file may be out of date, you should get new, up-to-date evidence from your doctors to take with you.

Before you receive the physical examination, you will be required to fill out a number of forms. One calls for information about illnesses and other medical conditions you have had in the past or now have, both physical and psychological. You should complete this form very carefully because the conditions you list on it are more likely to receive attention during the examination.

Since the examination may be hasty, you should point out to the doctors that you have evidence of a disqualifying condition, and if necessary be insistent that it be considered carefully.

During the examination you will also be required to fill out a form listing arrests and convictions. The AFEES can't find you acceptable for military service if you have been convicted of a felony (defined as a crime with a maximum penalty of more than a year in prison, regardless of how long you actually served), but the records of all men with serious criminal records are reviewed by a Moral Waiver Determination Board. This board evaluates the seriousness of the crime and the likelihood of rehabilitation to decide whether to consider you suitable for military service. In a recent year, it gave "moral waivers" to about two-thirds of those whose files it reviewed. If you were convicted of a felony and don't receive a moral waiver, you will be considered administratively (or "morally") unfit for the armed forces [AR 601-270, 23b]. If you have not been convicted of a felony but have a long police record for less serious crimes, you may sometimes be considered administratively unfit [AR 601-270, 23c] or medically unfit because of "personality disorders" [AR 40-501, 2-34a(1)].

If you are in the custody of a court (on bail while awaiting trial or on parole, for example), you cannot be found acceptable until you have an unconditional release from custody [AR 601-270, 23(d) and (e)].

Near the beginning of the examination you will also be asked to fill out and sign an Armed Forces Security Questionnaire (DD Form 98). This form consists of a list of nearly 300 organizations which have been declared subversive by the Attorney General, followed by a series of questions asking whether you have ever had any relationship to any of them (see form beginning on page 174). If you answer "yes" to any of the questions about affiliations, or if you qualify any answer, you will not be considered acceptable for military service until a security investigation has been completed [AR 601-270, 80b(2)], a process which may take a few weeks, several months, or ever longer.

The form indicates that you have a right to refuse to answer on Fifth Amendment grounds (possible self-incrimination), but most lawyers believe you have a right to refuse to answer questions about political affiliations even if you don't fear self-incrimination. Many people object to loyalty questionnaires because they see them as infringements of the Constitutional rights to freedom of association and belief guaranteed by the First Amendment. Refusal to answer the Armed Forces Security Questionnaire is not a violation of any law. A few draft boards have declared men delinquent for refusing to fill out this form, but the boards' actions were clearly illegal. If you refuse to answer these questions, you usually are asked to fill out a more detailed security questionnaire, and if you refuse to answer this one on the same grounds, you are asked (or "told") to submit to an interview with a military security official and "ordered" to submit to fingerprinting. You can decline to cooperate at all without breaking any law. If you persist in your refusal to answer questions about political affiliations, you will be subject to the same investigation as those who have given unsatisfactory answers. Only after the security investigation can you be found acceptable for military service.

In addition to those who refuse to answer on principle, some men refuse as a way to prolong the process and gain a little extra time, although they are usually warned that their refusal may keep them from getting security clearance for certain assignments if they later serve in the armed forces.

Most men who refuse to complete this form or who give "yes" answers are eventually found acceptable for military service, unless the investigation by military security officials reveals that they have been leaders or active members of organizations considered subversive, or have relatives in or other close ties to Communist countries which the armed forces consider would subject them to pressure to be disloyal [AR 604-10, 14].

Another part of the pre-induction examination is the Armed Forces Qualification Test, an aptitude and general

ARMED FORCES SECURITY QUESTIONNAIRE

I.—EXPLANATION

1. The interests of National Security require that all persons being considered for membership or retention in the Armed Forces be reliable, trustworthy, of good character, and of complete and unswerving loyalty to the United States. Accordingly, it is necessary for you to furnish information concerning your security qualifications. The answers which you give will be used in determining whether you are eligible for membership in the Armed Forces, in selection of your duty assignment, and for such other action as may be appropriate.

2. You are advised that in accordance with the Fifth Amendment of the Constitution of the United States you cannot be compelled to furnish any statements which you may reasonably believe may lead to your prosecution for a crime. This is the only reason for which you may avail yourself of the privilege afforded by the Fifth Amendment in refusing to answer questions under Part IV below. Claiming the Fifth Amendment will not by itself constitute sufficient grounds to exempt you from military service for reasons of security. You are not required to answer any questions in this questionnaire, the answer to which might be incriminating. If you do claim the privilege granted by the Fifth Amendment in refusing to answer any question, you should make a statement to that effect after the question involved.

II.—ORGANIZATIONS OF SECURITY SIGNIFICANCE

1. There is set forth below a list of names of organizations, groups, and movements, reported by the Attorney General of the United States as having significance in connection with the National Security. Please examine the list carefully, and note those organizations, and organizations of similar names, with which you are familiar. Then answer the questions set forth in Part IV below.

2. Your statement concerning membership or other association with one or more of the organizations named may not, of itself, cause you to be ineligible for acceptance or retention in the Armed Forces. Your age at the time of such association, circumstances prompting it, and the extent and frequency of involvement, are all highly pertinent, and will be fully weighed. Set forth all such factors under "Remarks" below, and continue on separate attached sheets of paper if necessary.

3. If there is any doubt in your mind as to whether your name has been linked with one of the organizations named, or as to whether a particular association is "worth mentioning," make a full explanation under "Remarks."

Organizations designated by the Attorney General, pursuant to Executive Order 10450, are listed below:

Communist Party, U. S. A., its subdivisions, subsidiaries and affiliates.

Communist Political Association, its subdivisions, subsidiaries and affiliates, including—
Alabama People's Educational Association.
Florida Press and Educational League.
Oklahoma League for Political Education.
People's Educational and Press Association of Texas.
Virginia League for People's Education.

Young Communist League.

American Slav Congress.
American Women for Peace.
American Youth Congress.
American Youth for Democracy.
Armenian Progressive League of America.
Associated Klans of America.
Association of Georgia Klans.
Association of German Nationals (*Reichsdeutsche Vereinigung*).
Ausland-Organization der NSDAP, Overseas Branch of Nazi Party.

Committee for a Democratic Far Eastern Policy.
Committee for Constitutional and Political Freedom.
Committee for the Defense of the Pittsburgh Six.
Committee for Nationalist Action.
Committee for the Negro in the Arts.
Committee for Peace and Brotherhood Festival in Philadelphia.
Committee for the Protection of the Bill of Rights.
Committee for World Youth Friendship and Cultural Exchange.
Committee to Defend Marie Richardson.

Abraham Lincoln Brigade.
Abraham Lincoln School, Chicago, Illinois.
Action Committee to Free Spain Now.
American Association for Reconstruction in Yugoslavia, Inc.
American Branch of the Federation of Greek Maritime Unions.
American Christian Nationalist Party.
American Committee for European Workers' Relief.
American Committee for Protection of Foreign Born.
American Committee for the Settlement of Jews in Birobidjan, Inc.
American Committee for Spanish Freedom.
American Committee for Yugoslav Relief, Inc.
American Committee to Survey Labor Conditions in Europe.
American Council for a Democratic Greece, formerly known as the Greek American Council; Greek American Committee for National Unity.
American Council on Soviet Relations.
American Croatian Congress.
American Jewish Labor Council.
American League Against War and Fascism.
American League for Peace and Democracy.
American National Labor Party.
American National Socialist League.
American National Socialist Party.
American Nationalist Party.
American Patriots, Inc.
American Peace Crusade.
American Peace Mobilization.
American Poles for Peace.
American Polish Labor Council.
American Polish League.
American Rescue Ship Mission (*a project of the United American Spanish Aid Committee*).
American-Russian Fraternal Society.
American-Russian Institute, New York (*also known as the American Russian Institute for Cultural Relations with the Soviet Union*).
American Russian Institute, Philadelphia.
American Russian Institute of San Francisco.
American Russian Institute of Southern California, Los Angeles.

Baltimore Forum.
Benjamin Davis Freedom Committee.
Black Dragon Society.
Boston School for Marxist Studies, Boston, Massachusetts.
Bridges-Robertson-Schmidt Defense Committee.
Bulgarian American People's League of the United States of America.

California Emergency Defense Committee.
California Labor School, Inc., 321 Divisadero Street, San Francisco, California.
Carpatho-Russian People's Society.
Central Council of American Women of Croatian Descent (*also known as Central Council of American Croatian Women, National Council of Croatian Women*).
Central Japanese Association (*Beikoku Chuo Nipponjin Kai*).
Central Japanese Association of Southern California.
Central Organization of the German-American National Alliance (*Deutsche-Amerikanische Einheitsfront*).
Cervantes Fraternal Society.
China Welfare Appeal, Inc.
Chopin Cultural Center.
Citizens Committee to Free Earl Browder.
Citizens Committee for Harry Bridges.
Citizens Committee of the Upper West Side (*New York City*).
Citizens Emergency Defense Conference.
Citizens Protective League.
Civil Liberties Sponsoring Committee of Pittsburgh.
Civil Rights Congress and its affiliated organizations, including Civil Rights Congress for Texas, Veterans Against Discrimination of Civil Rights Congress of New York.
Columbians.
Comite Coordinador Pro Republica Espanola.
Comite Pro Derechos Civiles.
Committee to Abolish Discrimination in Maryland.
Committee to Aid the Fighting South.
Committee to Defend the Rights and Freedom of Pittsburgh's Political Prisoners.

Commonwealth College, Mena, Arkansas.
Congress Against Discrimination.
Congress of the Unemployed.
Connecticut Committee to Aid Victims of the Smith Act.
Connecticut State Youth Conference.
Congress of American Revolutionary Writers.
Congress of American Women.
Council on African Affairs.
Council of Greek Americans.
Council for Jobs, Relief, and Housing.
Council for Pan-American Democracy.
Croatian Benevolent Fraternity.

Dai Nippon Butoku Kai (*Military Virtue Society of Japan or Military Art Society of Japan*).
Daily Worker Press Club.
Daniels Defense Committee.
Dante Alighieri Society (*Between 1935 and 1940*).
Dennis Defense Committee.
Detroit Youth Assembly.
East Bay Peace Committee.
Elsinore Progressive League.
Emergency Conference to Save Spanish Refuges (*founding body of the North American Spanish Aid Committee*).
Everybody's Committee to Outlaw War.

Families of the Baltimore Smith Act Victims.
Families of the Smith Act Victims.
Federation of Italian War Veterans in the U. S. A., Inc. (*Associazione Nazionale Combattenti Italiani, Federazione degli Stati Uniti d' America*).
Finnish-American Mutual Aid Society.
Florida Press and Educational League.
Frederick Douglass Educational Center.
Freedom Stage, Inc.
Friends of the New Germany (*Freunde des Neuen Deutschlands*).
Friends of the Soviet Union.

Garibaldi American Fraternal Society.
George Washington Carver School, New York City.
German-American Bund (*Amerikadeutscher Volksbund*).

German-American Republican League.
German-American Vocational League (*Deutsche-Amerikanische Berufsgemeinschaft*).
Guardian Club.

Harlem Trade Union Council.
Hawaii Civil Liberties Committee.
Heimuska Kai, also known as Nokubei Heieki, Gimusha Kai, Zaibei Nihonjin, Heyaku Gimusha Kai and Zaibei Heimusha Kai (*Japanese Residing in America Military Conscripts Association*).
Hellenic-American Brotherhood.
Hinode Kai (*Imperial Japanese Reservists*).
Hinomaru Kai (*Rising Sun Flag Society—a group of Japanese War Veterans*).
Hokubei Zaigo Shoke Dan (*North American Reserve Officers Association*).
Hollywood Writers Mobilization for Defense.
Hungarian-American Council for Democracy.
Hungarian Brotherhood.

Idaho Pension Union.
Independent Party (*Seattle, Washington*).
Independent Workers' Party.
Industrial Workers of the World.
International Labor Defense.
International Workers Order, its subdivisions, subsidiaries and affiliates.

Japanese Association of America.
Japanese Overseas Central Society (*Kaigai Dobo Chuo Kai*).
Japanese Overseas Convention, Tokyo, Japan, 1940.
Japanese Protective Association (*Recruiting Organization*).
Jefferson School of Social Science, New York City.
Jewish Culture Society.
Jewish People's Committee.
Jewish People's Fraternal Order.
Jikyoku Lin Kai (*The Committee for the Crisis*).
Johnson-Forest Group.
Johnsonites.
Joint Anti-Fascist Refugee Committee.
Joint Council of Progressive Italian-Americans, Inc.
Joseph Weydemeyer School of Social Science, St. Louis, Missouri.
Kibei Seinen Kai (*Association of U. S. citizens of Japanese ancestry who have returned to Japan for...*

Michigan Council for Peace.
Michigan School of Social Science.

Nanka Teikoku Gunyudan (*Imperial Military Friends Group or Southern California War Veterans*).
National Association of Mexican Americans (*also known as Asociacion Nacional Mexico-Americana*).
National Blue Star Mothers of America (not to be confused with the Blue Star Mothers of America organized in February 1942).
National Committee for the Defense of Political Prisoners.
National Committee for Freedom of the Press.
National Committee to Win Amnesty for Smith Act Victims.
National Committee to Win the Peace.
National Conference on American Policy in China and the Far East (*a Conference called by the Committee for a Democratic Far Eastern Policy*).
National Council of Americans of Croatian Descent.
National Council of American-Soviet Friendship.
National Federation for Constitutional Liberties.
National Labor Conference for Peace.
National Negro Congress.
National Negro Labor Council.
Nationalist Action League.
Nationalist Party of Puerto Rico.
Nature Friends of America (*Since 1935*).
Negro Labor Victory Committee.
New Committee for Publications.
Nichibei Kogyo Kaisha (*The Great Fujii Theatre*).
North American Committee to Aid Spanish Democracy.
North Philadelphia Forum.
Northwest Japanese Association.

Ohio School of Social Sciences.
Oklahoma Committee to Defend Political Prisoners.
Oklahoma League for Political Education.
Original Southern Klans, Incorporated.

Pacific Northwest Labor School, Seattle, Washington.
Palo Alto Peace Club.
Partido del Pueblo of Panama (*operating in the Canal Zone*).
Peace Information Center.
Peace Movement of Ethiopia.

Puertorriquenos Unidos (*Puerto Ricans United*).

Quad City Committee for Peace.
Queensbridge Tenants League.

Revolutionary Workers League.
Romanian-American Fraternal Society.
Russian American Society, Inc.

Sakura Kai (*Patriotic Society, or Cherry Association, composed of veterans of Russo-Japanese War*).
Samuel Adams School, Boston, Mass.
Santa Barbara Peace Forum.
Schappes Defense Committee.
Schneiderman-Darcy Defense Committee.
School of Jewish Studies, New York City.
Seattle Labor School, Seattle, Washington.
Serbian-American Fraternal Society.
Serbian Vidovdan Council.
Shinto Temples (Limited to State Shinto abolished in 1945).
Silver Shirt Legion of America.
Slavic Council of Southern California.
Slovak Workers Society.
Slovenian-American National Council
Socialist Workers Party, including American Committee for European Workers Relief.
Sokoku Kai (*Fatherland Society*).
Southern Negro Youth Congress.
Suiko Sha (*Reserve Officers Association, Los Angeles*).
Syracuse Women for Peace.

Tom Paine School of Social Science, Philadelphia, Pennsylvania.
Tom Paine School of Westchester, New York.
Trade Union Committee for Peace.
Trade Unionists for Peace.
Tri-State Negro Trade Union Council.

Ukrainian-American Fraternal Union.
Union of American Croatians.
Union of New York Veterans.
United American Spanish Aid Committee.
United Committee of Jewish Societies and Landsmanschaft Federations, also known as Coordination Committee of Jewish Landsmanschaften and Fraternal Organizations.
United Committee of South Slavic Americans.

studying in Japan).
Knights of the White Camelia.
Ku Klux Klan.
Kyffhaeuser, also known as Kyffhaeuser League (Kyffhaeuser Bund), Kyffhaeuser Fellowship (Kyffhaeuser Kameradschaft).
Kyffhaeuser War Relief (Kyffhaeuser Kriegshilfswerk).
Labor Council for Negro Rights.
Labor Research Association, Inc.
Labor Youth League.
League for Common Sense.
League of American Writers.
Lictor Society (Italian Black Shirts).
Macedonian-American People's League.
Mario Morgantini Circle.
Maritime Labor Committee to Defend Al Lannon.
Maryland Congress Against Discrimination.
Massachusetts Committee for the Bill of Rights.
Massachusetts Minute Women for Peace (not connected with the Minute Women of the U. S. A. Inc.).
Maurice Braverman Defense Committee.
Michigan Civil Rights Federation.

People's Educational and Press Association of Texas.
People's Educational Association (Incorporated under name Los Angeles Educational Association, Inc.), also known as People's Educational Center, People's University, People's School.
People's Institute of Applied Religion.
Peoples Programs (Seattle, Washington).
People's Radio Foundation, Inc.
People's Rights Party.
Philadelphia Labor Committee for Negro Rights.
Philadelphia School of Social Science and Art.
Photo League (New York City).
Pittsburgh Arts Club.
Political Prisoners' Welfare Committee.
Polonia Society of the IWO.
Progressive German-Americans, also known as Progressive German-Americans of Chicago.
Proletarian Party of America.
Protestant War Veterans of the United States, Inc.
Provisional Committee of Citizens for Peace, Southwest Area.
Provisional Committee on Latin American Affairs.
Provisional Committee to Abolish Discrimination in the State of Maryland.
Puerto Rican Comite Pro Liberades Civiles (CLC).

United Harlem Tenants and Consumers Organization.
United May Day Committee.
United Negro and Allied Veterans of America.
Veterans Against Discrimination of Civil Rights Congress of New York.
Veterans of the Abraham Lincoln Brigade.
Virginia League for People's Education.
Voice of Freedom Committee.
Walt Whitman School of Social Science, Newark, New Jersey.
Washington Bookshop Association.
Washington Committee to Defend the Bill of Rights.
Washington Committee for Democratic Action.
Washington Commonwealth Federation.
Washington Pension Union.
Wisconsin Conference on Social Legislation.
Workers Alliance (June April 1936).
Yiddisher Kultur Farband.
Yugoslav-American Cooperative Home, Inc.
Yugoslav Seamen's Club, Inc.

III.—INSTRUCTIONS

1. Set forth an explanation for each answer checked "Yes" under question 2 below under "Remarks." Attach as many extra sheets as necessary for a full explanation, signing or initialing each extra sheet.

2. Title 18, U. S. Code, Section 1001, provides, in pertinent part: "Whoever . . . falsifies, conceals or covers up . . . a material fact, or makes any false . . . statements . . . or makes or uses any false writing . . . shall be fined not more than $10,000 or imprisoned not more than 5 years, or both." Any false, fraudulent or fictitious response to the questions under Part IV below may give rise to criminal liability under Title 18, U. S. C. Section 1001. You are advised, however, that you will not incur such liability unless you supply inaccurate statements with knowledge of their untruthfulness. You are therefore advised that before you sign this form and turn it in to Selective Service or military authorities, you should be sure that it is truthful; that detailed explanations are given for each "Yes" answer under question 2 of Part IV below, and that details given are as full and complete as you can make them.

3. In stating details, it is permissible, if your memory is hazy on particular points, to use such expressions as, "I think," "in my opinion," "I believe," or "to the best of my recollection."

C48—77820-1

IV.—QUESTIONS

(For each answer checked "Yes" under question 2, set forth a full explanation under "Remarks" below)

	YES	NO
1. I have read the list of names of organizations, groups, and movements set forth under Part II of this form and the explanation which precedes it.		
2. Concerning the list of organization, groups and movements set forth under Part II above:		
a. Are you now a member of any of the organizations, groups, or movements listed?		
b. Have you ever been a member of any of the organizations, groups, or movements listed?		
c. Are you now employed by any of the organizations, groups, or movements listed?		
d. Have you ever been employed by any of the organizations, groups, or movements listed?		
e. Have you ever attended any meeting of any of the organizations, groups, or movements listed?		
f. Have you ever attended any social gathering of any of the organizations, groups, or movements listed?		
g. Have you ever attended any gathering of any kind sponsored by any of the organizations, groups, or movements listed?		
h. Have you prepared material for publication by any of the organizations, groups, or movements listed?		
i. Have you ever contributed money to any of the organizations, groups, or movements listed?		
k. Have you ever contributed services to any of the organizations, groups, or movements listed?		
l. Have you ever subscribed to any publication of any of the organizations, groups, or movements listed?		
m. Have you ever been employed by a foreign government or any agency thereof?		
n. Are you now a member of the Communist Party of any foreign country?		
o. Have you ever been a member of the Communist Party of any foreign country?		
p. Have you ever been the subject of a loyalty or security hearing?		
q. Are you now or have you ever been a member of any organization, association, movement, group or combination of persons not on the Attorney General's list which advocates the overthrow of our constitutional form of government, or which has adopted the policy of advocating or approving the commission of acts of force or violence to deny other persons their rights under the Constitution of the United States, or which seeks to alter the form of government of the United States by unconstitutional means?		

178

i. Have you ever corresponded with any of the organizations, groups, or movements listed or with any publication thereof?

r. Have you ever been known by any other last name than that used in signing this questionnaire?

REMARKS

CERTIFICATION

In regard to any part of this questionnaire concerning which I have had any question as to the meaning, I have requested and have obtained a complete explanation. I certify that the statements made by me under Part IV above and on any supplemental pages hereto attached, are full, true, and correct.

TYPED FULL NAME OF PERSON MAKING CERTIFICATION	SERVICE NUMBER (If any)	SIGNATURE OF PERSON MAKING CERTIFICATION
TYPED NAME OF WITNESS	DATE	SIGNATURE OF WITNESS

C48—77620-1   ☆ GPO 1966 O—222-748

Page 4

information test to determine your mental acceptability. If you fail this test, you are given further mental tests, and your educational background is considered to determine whether you have failed deliberately. High school graduates are usually considered acceptable even if they fail the mental tests [AR 601-270, 58 and 59].

During the 1967 fiscal year, almost 400,000 men, or 37.1% of those sent for pre-induction physical examinations, were found unacceptable, about two-thirds of them for medical reasons and the rest for mental or administrative reasons.

At the conclusion of the examination, your local board will be notified of the results and will receive copies of all the forms containing the details of the examination. Since these are in your file, you are able to examine and copy them if you wish (see pages 13 and 49 for details of your right to examine your file). The local board must notify you officially of the results by sending you a Statement of Acceptability (DD Form 62), illustrated on page 76, which must indicate whether you were found acceptable or unacceptable.

However, even before this official notification, you should know whether you passed the pre-induction physical examination because the regulations require that the AFEES officials tell you before you leave [AR 601-270, 27]. Therefore, if you are told that you have been found acceptable but believe you should have been disqualified, you should take action immediately as suggested below.

AFTER THE PRE-INDUCTION EXAMINATION

Selective Service Regulations do not permit you to appeal the results of a pre-induction physical examination unless it results in a change in your classification, and even then the usual personal appearance and appeal rights are unlikely to gain recognition of a medical condition, though they may be useful as a way to protect you from induction while you try other means to have the evaluation changed. Most men are already classified I-A before they take the examination, so no Selective Service appeal is possible.

However, it is possible to use unofficial but sometimes effective appeal procedures to get further consideration of medical claims, not through Selective Service but by writing to the Army.

If you and your doctor disagree with the results of your pre-induction physical examination, you should write immediately to The Surgeon, U.S. Army Recruiting Command, Hampton, Virginia 23369. You should explain in your letter why you believe the decision at the AFEES was in error and enclose a copy of your medical evidence. If your claim is convincing, you will be given a more thorough examination.

If you are not satisfied with the results of your appeal to The Surgeon, you can write to Chief, Physical Standards Division, Office of the Surgeon General, Department of the Army, Washington, D.C. 20315. Again you must explain why your condition needs further evaluation and enclose a copy of the medical evidence.

Needless to say, letters should be sent to these officials only if your condition is genuine and you have good evidence, for they will be less inclined to intervene in cases of genuine need if they receive many false or unconvincing requests.

EXAMINATION AT INDUCTION

A complete armed forces physical examination is valid for one year. Your local board can issue an induction order even if you passed the examination more than a year ago, or if you are a draft delinquent or a volunteer for induction and have never had a pre-induction examination, but on the day of induction you must be given a complete examination.

If your pre-induction physical examination was taken less than a year ago, you do not receive the complete examination but are given a "physical inspection" on the day of induction. This is a much less complete check, but if you have submitted new evidence of a disqualifying condition it should be carefully considered [AR 601-270, 69].

The Armed Forces Security Questionnaire (DD Form 98) is valid for only 120 days, and you will be asked to answer it again if your pre-induction examination was taken longer than four months before your induction date. If you refuse to answer it, or give any "yes" or qualified answers and refuse to provide additional security information, you shouldn't be inducted until a security investigation has been completed [AR 601-270, 80b(2)]. You will also be asked to fill out a more detailed security questionnaire, the Statement of Personal History (DD Form 398), which is usually sent to you by your local board with the induction order, but refusing to answer it will not necessarily delay your induction.

During fiscal year 1967, over 47,000 men, or 13.6% of those ordered for induction, were found unacceptable at the point of induction.

IF YOU ARE FOUND UNACCEPTABLE

Occasionally a man who wants to get into the armed forces is rejected at the physical examination and wants to appeal the decision. If this is your desire, you should use the unofficial appeal procedures described above, enclosing doctors' letters showing that you do not have the condition for which you were rejected or that it is not serious enough to interfere with military duty.

Many, perhaps most, men who are rejected are pleased to be excused from military duty. When the local board receives the notice from the AFEES that you were found unacceptable, it should reclassify you I-Y or IV-F at its next meeting unless you have become eligible for a lower classification. Sometimes the AFEES suggests that you should be returned in a few months for another examination, but you should still be reclassified so that you will have full appeal rights if you are later re-examined and found acceptable.

No Selective Service classification is necessarily permanent. New evidence or a change of circumstances can always result in reclassification. Men classified I-Y or IV-F can be sent for another examination at any time, though repeat examinations are much more common in I-Y than IV-F.

If you are found unacceptable at an armed forces physical examination but the doctors believe your disqualification is temporary, they must still reject you [AR 601-270, 70d], but will usually tell your local board to send you for another examination at a specified time, often after three or six months. You cannot receive an induction order during this time and your board should classify you I-Y or IV-F. You must first take and pass another pre-induction examination, and receive a new Statement of Acceptability, before an induction order can be issued. Before sending you for a new examination, your local board may send you for an interview with its medical advisor to decide whether you are likely to pass the new examination [LBM 78]. Of course, you cannot be found acceptable merely on the advice of the medical advisor. If he considers you acceptable, you are sent for another examination at the AFEES. You will receive a complete physical examination if your previous examination was more than a year earlier, or a "physical inspection" if it was less than a year earlier. If you are found acceptable, your local board is notified and will usually reclassify you from I-Y or IV-F at its next meeting. You have full Selective Service appeal rights as well as the chance to use the unofficial appeal processes described above.

PART IV

CONSCIENTIOUS OBJECTION

"Nothing contained in this title shall be construed to require any person to be subject to combatant training and service in the armed forces of the United States who, by reason of religious training and belief, is conscientiously opposed to participation in war in any form. As used in this subsection, the term 'religious training and belief' does not include essentially political, sociological, or philosophical views, or a merely personal moral code. Any person claiming exemption from combatant training and service because of such conscientious objections whose claim is sustained by the local board shall, if he is inducted into the armed forces under this title, be assigned to noncombatant service as defined by the President, or shall, if he is found to be conscientiously opposed to participation in such noncombatant service, in lieu of such induction, be ordered by his local board, subject to such regulations as the President may prescribe, to perform for a period equal to the period prescribed in section 4(b) such civilian work contributing to the maintenance of the national health, safety, or interest as the local board pursuant to Presidential regulations may deem appropriate and any such person who knowingly fails or neglects to obey any such order from his local board shall be deemed, for the purposes of section 12 of this title, to have knowingly failed or neglected to perform a duty required of him under this title."

MILITARY SELECTIVE SERVICE ACT OF 1967, 6(j)

CHAPTER FOURTEEN

APPLYING AS A CONSCIENTIOUS OBJECTOR

In simplest terms, you are a conscientious objector (CO) if you are strongly opposed to participating in war. If you apply for a CO classification and your local board accepts your claim, you will be drafted at the usual time if you don't qualify for a deferment but must be assigned to a special form of service.

There are two classifications for conscientious objectors. If you have strong moral objections to killing in war and to carrying arms, you should apply for the I-A-O classification; as a I-A-O you may be drafted into the Army but must be assigned to noncombatant duty—usually the Army Medical Corps. If you are morally opposed to any form of military service, for example because you view even Army medics as contributing to the war-making job of the Army, you should apply for the I-O classification; as a I-O you may be ordered to spend two years in civilian alternate service approved by your local board—work "contributing to the maintenance of the national health, safety, or interest." These two types of service are discussed in Chapter 15.

Whether you apply for a I-A-O or a I-O classification, you must meet three requirements to be recognized as a CO. First, your objction must be based on "religious training and belief." Second, you must be "opposed to participation in war in any form." Third, your claim must be sincere. The remainder of this chapter discusses these three qualifications and the procedure for applying as a CO.

RELIGIOUS TRAINING AND BELIEF

"Religious training and belief" isn't defined in the law except in a negative way: the term "does not include essentially political, sociological, or philosophical views, or a merely personal moral code."

Until 1967, the law defined the term as "an individual's belief in a relation to a Supreme Being involving duties superior to those arising from any human relation." This language was removed from the 1967 law, and the 1968 revision of the Special Form for Conscientious Objector (Form 150) removed the questions about belief in a Supreme Being (see form, page 194). Therefore, it is necessary to turn to court decisions to learn the meaning of "religious training and belief."

In 1965, the Supreme Court, in *U.S. v. Seeger* (380 U.S. 163), discussed the meaning of "religious training and belief" and offered a very broad definition:

Within that phrase would come all sincere religious beliefs which are based upon a power or being, or upon a faith, to which all else is subordinate or upon which all else is ultimately dependent. The test might be stated in these words: A sincere and meaningful belief which occupies in the life of its possessor a place parallel to that filled by the God of those admittedly qualifying for the exemption comes within the statutory definition.

Even before the Seeger decision you didn't have to base your claim on membership in a church or on a conventional belief in God. But since Seeger was an agnostic, the decision made it clear that any belief or value which you live by, which is so basic to your own thinking that it is your personal religion, can lead you to be a CO and will meet the legal requirement.

This definition of "religious training and belief" is so broad that it would be hard to think of any sincere CO who doesn't qualify. Every person lives by some beliefs, some set of basic values, though it may be hard to put them into words.

What about the exclusion of "essentially political, sociological, or philosophical views, or a merely personal moral code"? The important words seem to be "essentially" and "merely." In the Seeger decision, the Supreme Court said, "The use by Congress of the words 'merely personal' seems to us to restrict the exception to a moral code which is not only personal but which is the sole basis for the registrant's belief. . . ." It is difficult to be sure just what this means, but it seems clear that if your belief is basic enough to your thinking that you consider it religious, you could qualify for the CO classification. Your belief can probably be considered nonreligious only if you insist that it is not religious—even in the very broad sense of the Seeger decision—but entirely personal.

Similarly, you probably have political, sociological, or philosophical views, but you can't base your claim on them. Nor can your claim be denied because of them, unless they contradict your CO claim. If you live by certain values, these are basic and your political, sociological, or philosophical views reflect these more basic beliefs. You should be turned down only if your beliefs are not at all religious—again, as broadly defined—but entirely political, sociological, or philosophical (*Fleming v. U.S.,* 344 F.2d 912, 1965).

PARTICIPATION IN WAR IN ANY FORM

The Selective Service System generally interprets the "participation in war in any form" requirement to mean that a CO must be opposed to all war. Therefore, it would not give you a CO classification if you expressed a willingness to fight in some wars but not in others.

Court decisions have indicated that a CO doesn't have to be opposed to all violence, however. If you believe in self-defense, or the defense of your family, or would use violence if necessary to protect a friend from attack, you can still be recognized as a CO if you are opposed to war (*Sicurella v. U.S.*, 348 U.S. 385, 1955). In other words, you don't have to be a pacifist, as that word is ordinarily used.

Although Selective Service interprets the law to require that you be opposed to all war, it should be pointed out that the law is phrased in the present tense: "any person . . . who . . . *is* conscientiously opposed. . . ." And the statement you sign on the Special Form for Conscientious Objector (Form 150) starts, "I *am,* by reason of my religious training and belief, conscientiously opposed. . . ." Therefore, it seems to many lawyers, it is not necessary to decide whether you might have fought in a past war or whether you may feel differently about a future or hypothetical war. If you had been alive and old enough for military service at the time of World War II, the Civil War, or the American Revolution, you would have been a different person, formed by different experiences. Similarly, to make up your mind whether you would fight in some future war, you would need to know today how you will feel at a future date. How can you know what information, experiences, and convictions would influence you then? All that seems necessary under the present law is to decide whether you, the actual you, can participate in the real wars of today.

However, if you are sure that you can fight in war under some foreseeable circumstances but not others, you are not likely to receive a CO classification.

Many Western religions teach a "just war" concept, requiring a moral judgment about the particular war you are faced with, and usually setting up a basis for making the judgment. If this is your position, and you have examined modern war by these standards, you may conclude that war can no longer be just, and therefore that you can't participate without violating your beliefs. You may well not be considered eligible for a CO classification by Selective Service. The law, as now interpreted, does not make provision for the "unjust war" or "selective" objector, though some lawyers believe that the wording of the law will cause courts to make a broader interpretation. Thus far, however, this question has been avoided by the courts. No decision has ever been based specifically on this issue, and therefore it is impossible to say whether the selective objector position will ultimately be upheld or turned down. It is safe to say, however, that the Selective Service System rejects this interpretation and will turn down your application if you indicate that you are opposed to some wars but not to all.

SINCERITY

If you claim to be opposed to war by reason of your religious beliefs, your draft board will decide whether in its opinion you are sincere—that is, whether you are telling the truth. It can't turn down your claim merely because it is doubtful or feels you haven't "proved" it. It is hard to explain religious convictions and harder still to "prove" you hold them. Therefore, courts have ruled that a CO claim can't arbitrarily be turned down by a skeptical draft board (*Dickinson v. U.S.,* 346 U.S. 389, 1953). Only on the basis of facts in the individual's file which indicate that his claim might be insincere will a federal court uphold the rejection of a CO claim.

The board will use your answers to Form 150, discussed below, to try to decide whether your claim is sincere. It should also consider the letters of support you have submitted, anything said by you and your witnesses at a personal appearance and all other evidence offered by you or others. Before 1967, there was provision in the law for a hearing and an FBI investigation as part of the appeal procedure, to collect information about your sincerity, but this is no longer done. The local board has the power to contact your references, call witnesses, and ask welfare or governmental agencies to supply information, but these powers are very rarely used in CO claims outside the state of Washington. As a result, nearly all of the information the board will have comes from you and those you ask to give information about you.

WHEN TO APPLY

The local board must send you a copy of the Special Form for Conscientious Objector (Form 150) whenever you request it [REG 1621.11]. It is certainly best, however, to apply as soon as you realize that you are a CO. In fact, the requirement that you notify your board within 10 days of new information that could affect your classification makes it a legal obligation to apply as a CO as soon as you decide that you cannot conscientiously become a member of the armed forces.

Even if it were not required, it would be sensible to apply as early as possible, to reduce the board's suspicion that your claim was made just because you expected to be drafted into the Army. There is little danger in applying early. Even if you still need to refine your thinking, the CO claim should be made; you can add more complete answers or better evidence at any time.

Filing a CO claim doesn't keep you from receiving or keeping any deferments you are entitled to. The board is required to put you into the lowest classification for which you are eligible, and all deferments are lower than the two CO classifications. Your local board shouldn't even consider the CO application as long as you are deferred. Some men suspect that the board may be unwilling to give an occupational or hardship-to-dependents deferment, or some other deferment granted at the discretion of the board, if they have filed CO claims, and this does occasionally happen. But more often boards seem to prefer to give COs such deferments to put off the necessity of deciding about the CO claim.

The first chance to make a CO claim is when you file the Classification Questionnaire (Form 100), normally at age 18 (see Chapter 4). If you sign Series VIII, the Form 150 should be mailed to you promptly, though sometimes a letter must be sent to remind the board to mail it.

If you don't claim to be a CO when you answer the Classification Questionnaire, any CO claim made after that is considered a "late claim." It must still be considered, but you will need to explain how your beliefs have developed or matured since you filed the Classification Questionnaire. From the board's point of view, not signing Series VIII on that form indicates you were not a CO at that time.

Even a CO claim made after the board has sent you an induction order must be given some consideration, but these are the hardest claims to get recognized. To get a reopening of your classification at this point, you will probably have to convince the board that your beliefs crystallized or matured only *after* your board issued the induction order (*U.S. v. Gearey,* 368 F.2d 144), and therefore that your late claim represents "a change in the registrant's status resulting from circumstances over which the registrant had no control" [REG 1625.2]. Anyone who decides to make a CO claim after he has received an induction order needs the help of a very experienced counselor or attorney.

Form approved.
Budget Bureau No. 33-RO115

SELECTIVE SERVICE SYSTEM
SPECIAL FORM FOR CONSCIENTIOUS OBJECTOR

(Local Board Stamp)

┌─ DATE QUESTIONNAIRE RECEIVED
    AT LOCAL BOARD ─┐

Date of Mailing ....

Complete and return within 30 days.

1. Name of Registrant (First)	(Middle)	(Last)

2. Selective Service No.

3. Mailing address (Number and street, city, county and State, and ZIP Code)

(The above items, except the date received back at local board, are to be filled in by the local board before the questionnaire is mailed.)

INSTRUCTIONS

A registrant who claims to be a conscientious objector shall offer information in substantiation of his claim on this special form which, when filed, shall become a part of his Classification Questionnaire (SSS Form 100).

Section 6(j) of the Military Selective Service Act of 1967 provides:

"Nothing contained in this title shall be construed to require any person to be subject to combatant training and service in the Armed Forces of the United States who, by reason of religious training and belief, is conscientiously opposed to participation in war in any form. As used in this subsection, the term 'religious training and belief' does not include essentially political, sociological, or philosophical views, or a merely personal moral code. Any person claiming exemption from combatant training and service because of such conscientious objections whose claim is sustained by the local board shall, if he is inducted into the Armed Forces under this title, be assigned to noncombatant service as defined by the President, or shall, if he is found to be conscientiously opposed to participation in such noncombatant service, in lieu of such induction, be ordered by his local board, subject to such regulations as the President may prescribe, to perform for a period equal to the period prescribed in section 4(b) such civilian work contributing to the maintenance of the national health, safety, or interest as the local board pursuant to Presidential regulations may deem appropriate and any such person who knowingly fails or neglects to obey any such order from his local board shall be deemed, for the purposes of section 12 of this title, to have knowingly failed or neglected to perform a duty required of him under this title."

SSS Form 150 (Revised 8-30-68). (Previous Printings Obsolete)

(1)

Series I.—CLAIM FOR EXEMPTION

INSTRUCTIONS.—The registrant should sign his name to either statement A or B in this series. If he cannot sign either one, he must indicate why.

A I am, by reason of my religious training and belief, conscientiously opposed to participation in war in any form. I, therefore, claim exemption from combatant training and service in the Armed Forces, but am prepared to serve in a noncombatant capacity if called. (Registrants granted this status are classified I–A–O.)

_____

(Signature of registrant)

B I am, by reason of my religious training and belief, conscientiously opposed to participation in war in any form and I am further conscientiously opposed to participation in noncombatant training and service in the Armed Forces. I, therefore, claim exemption from both combatant and noncombatant training and service in the Armed Forces, but am prepared to perform civilian alternative service if called. (Registrants granted this status are classified I–O.)

_____

(Signature of registrant)

Series II.—RELIGIOUS TRAINING AND BELIEF

INSTRUCTIONS.—If more space is needed use extra sheets of paper.

1. Describe the nature of your belief which is the basis of your claim and state why you consider it to be based on religious training and belief.

196

2. Explain how, when and from whom or from what source you received the religious training and acquired the religious belief which is the basis of your claim. (Include here, where applicable, such information as religion of parents and other members of family; childhood religious training; religious and general education; experiences at school and college; organizational memberships and affiliations; books and other readings which influenced you; association with clergymen, teachers, advisers or other individuals which affected you; and any other material which will help give the local board the fullest possible picture of how your beliefs developed.)

(2)

197

3. To what extent does your religious training and belief restrict you from ministering to the sick and injured, either civilian or military, or from serving in the Armed Forces as a noncombatant without weapons?

----

4. Have you ever given expression publicly or privately, written or oral, to the views herein expressed as the basis for your claim? Give examples.

Series III.—REFERENCES

You may provide your local board with any additional evidence from any source that would support your claim of conscientious objection. You may, if you choose, provide in the space below the names of references who could provide the local board with information regarding your religious training and belief. You may wish to suggest that these references, if given, write directly to the local board in support of your claim.

NAME	FULL ADDRESS	OCCUPATION OR POSITION	RELATIONSHIP TO YOU

(3)

REGISTRANT'S CERTIFICATE

INSTRUCTIONS.—Every registrant claiming to be a conscientious objector shall make this certificate.

NOTICE.—Imprisonment for not more than 5 years or a fine of not more than $10,000, or both such fine and imprisonment, is provided by law as a penalty for knowingly making or being a party to the making of any false statement or certificate regarding or bearing upon a classification. (Military Selective Service Act of 1967.)

I, _____, certify that I am the registrant named and described in the foregoing statements in this form; that I have read (or have had read to me) the statements made by and about me, and that each and every such statement is true and complete to the best of my knowledge, information, and belief. The statements made by me in the foregoing _____ (are, are not) in my own handwriting.

Registrant sign here 👉 _____
                                          (Signature or mark of registrant)

_____
(Date)

_____
(Signature of witness to mark of registrant)

_____
(Date)

If another person has assisted the registrant in completing this form, such person shall sign the following statement:

I have assisted the registrant herein named in completing this form.

_____
(Signature of person who has assisted)

_____
(Occupation of person who has assisted)

_____
(Address of person who has assisted)

_____
(Date)

(4)

U.S. GOVERNMENT PRINTING OFFICE: 1968—O-318-764

FILLING OUT FORM 150

Answering the questions on Form 150 is difficult. It involves trying to put into words the values by which you live—never an easy task. It is made harder in this case because you are explaining your beliefs to the members of your draft board, who are fairly certain not only to have entirely different beliefs but to be unhappy about those who disagree with them. Therefore, it is important that you try to write clearly, simply, and carefully.

Once you send for the Form 150, you are given 30 days to fill it out and return it. Although that's better than the 10 days allowed before the fall of 1968, it still isn't usually long enough to think out your beliefs, write your answers, discuss them with a counselor, and revise them, and at the same time to collect supporting letters from references. Therefore, it's a good idea to start your thinking, writing, and discussing before you actually receive the form, and if possible even before you send for it. A copy of the Form 150 begins on page 194.

The form consists of three important parts.

In Series I, you are asked to sign one of two statements to indicate whether you are claiming a I-A-O or a I-O classification. If you can't sign either statement for some reason, you must explain why. Whatever the explanation, it is not likely to cause your draft board to classify you either I-A-O or I-O.

Series II asks four questions about your beliefs.

Question 1 should be answered with a concise essay on the basic beliefs you live by, why you think they are religious (in the broad sense of the Seeger decision), and why they lead you to be a CO. You are not expected to confine your answers to the few lines on the form; most applicants type their essays on separate sheets and write "see attached pages" on the form. Don't be long-winded, but give a full description of your beliefs as they relate to participation in war.

It is neither necessary nor helpful to discuss side issues. If you are opposed to war because you oppose all violence, it is useful to say so. If you believe in violence in defense of yourself and your family, but oppose the organized, massive violence of war, concentrate on your reasons for opposing war. The 1968 form, unlike the earlier one, doesn't ask for a complete discussion of your attitude toward the use of force, and there is usually no need to offer one. If you aren't sure what you would have done during past wars, you don't need to discuss them. You should, however, be prepared for such hypothetical questions at your personal appearance later.

Question 2 asks how your beliefs developed. The best answer is usually a chronological description of the development of your thinking on the subject, mentioning the influences and experiences along the way that brought you to your present position. This may be fairly short if you are 18 years old and base your claim on family or church background. If you are older, or if your beliefs are less conventional, this personal history should be more detailed, especially if you gave no hint of being a CO on your Classification Questionnaire. If you are applying at age 24 or 25, or after receiving an induction order, you will need a very complete history to show why your beliefs reached maturity at this time.

Question 3 asks whether, and if so why, you are unable to be a soldier in the Army Medical Corps or to serve as a civilian in a hospital. I-A-Os usually serve in the Medical Corps. I-Os often serve in civilian hospitals. If you are applying as a I-O, you will need to explain why noncombatant military service would conflict with your beliefs. In this case, it may be helpful to think about the purpose of the service as well as the specific duties. Of course, you should show how this thinking relates to your religious beliefs as described in Question 1.

Question 4 gives you a chance to show that you try to live according to your beliefs—that you are sincere. Have your values caused you to enter into social service, religious work, anti-war or civil rights activity? Have your beliefs influenced your choice of work or study? How have you dealt with situations that might have involved violence? Have you expressed your developing beliefs in term papers, letters, discussions, meetings, or even more public ways? A picture of a man struggling to live according to his beliefs should emerge.

Series III givs you a chance to add more evidence of sincerity. You may be able to attach school papers, newspaper clippings, speeches, or other items by or about you which illustrate that you sincerely try to express and live your beliefs. You certainly should send letters written by people who know you well—friends, clergyman, teachers, family friends, neighbors, employers, and even members of your family. These letters should attest to the fact that you are sincerely opposed to all war for religious reasons. The instructions on the form suggest that the letters should be sent directly to the draft board, and some local boards may therefore expect this to be done. However, many men will prefer to have the letters returned to them for screening and copying, and to send them with the Form 150, and this is not forbidden. Not all well-motivated references write helpful letters, so it may be wise to examine the letters before they are sent in and to use only those that will help your claim. Draft boards rarely write to your references, so it will be up to you to get letters. Although only five spaces are given, you will probably want to get more letters than that. Some counselors suggest about eight good letters; if you submit more, they are less ikely to be read carefully by the members of your draft board.

You must sign and date the certificate section at the end. A witness is required only if you are illiterate and must sign with a cross. A draft counselor must sign that he assisted you only if he worded your answers.

AFTER FORM 150 IS SUBMITTED

After you have returned your Form 150, your work is not done. A recent memorandum from the national director of Selective Service [LBM 41] suggests that your board ask you to attend a meeting before it decides whether to approve your claim. You should follow the suggestions in Chapter 5, on preparing for a personal appearance, with great care, and try to take a witness. This meeting doesn't count as a personal appearance, so if the board gives you an unacceptable classification you can still have a personal appearance and try again to convince the board that your claim is sincere. More evidence can be submitted at any time.

For a detailed discussion of the Form 150 and the meaning of the CO provisions in the Selective Service law, read the *Handbook for Conscientious Objectors* published by the Central Committee for Conscientious Objectors (see Chapter 21). It is especially important that you have the help of a draft counselor if you are making a CO claim.

It is also important that you think carefully about what you believe and how strongly you believe it, for you may have to show great persistence to be recognized as a CO. Local boards, and even appeal boards, often ignore court decisions and reject CO claims for improper reasons, and some COs have had to write to Selective Service state directors and other officials, or even to refuse induction and face the risks of trial, before their claims were recognized.

Despite this apparent arbitrariness and unpredictability, the Central Committee for Conscientious Objectors reports, as this book goes to press, that it knows of no man now in prison who sought recognition as a CO before receiving an induction order and used all appeals open to him.

CHAPTER FIFTEEN

NONCOMBATANT MILITARY SERVICE AND
CIVILIAN ALTERNATE SERVICE: I-A-O, I-O, I-W

Just as conscientious objectors have the same rights of deferment as other men, they have the same obligation to serve if called. If you get one of the two CO classifications, you will be drafted at the same age and have to serve for the same two years as a man classified I-A. The difference is that you will be ordered to do a different type of service, intended to be consistent with your beliefs as a CO.

NONCOMBATANT MILITARY SERVICE: I-A-O

If you apply for a I-A-O classification, you are saying in effect, "I object to killing or carrying arms, but am willing to serve in the armed forces, wear the uniform, and obey all orders which don't involve my using weapons." If you receive this classification and are inducted into the Army, you will receive your basic training at the Medical Training Center, Fort Sam Houston, San Antonio, Texas. You will receive roughly the same basic training as other soldiers, but without any weapons training. After basic training, you will receive individual training—probably as a "medical aidman." About 99% of all I-A-Os are assigned as medics, and the remainder serve as cooks, clerks, truck drivers, chaplains' assistants, and in other noncombatant assignments.

As a medic, you may perform acts of mercy, saving life, easing suffering, and preventing sickness, and you may sometimes be able to serve civilians in war zones as well as soldiers. You may find this period of service valuable and satisfying, and you are likely to be respected and depended upon by the combat soldiers you serve with. Men classified I-A-O provide about 6% to 8% of the Army's medical aidmen. You are just as likely to be sent into a combat area and to be placed on the front lines as a medic who isn't a CO, and you are actually more likely to be sent into combat than a I-A.

However, do not enter military service as a I-A-O imagining that the medics are somehow separate from the Army and its basic purpose. This view is contradicted by the Army: "The primary duty of medical troops as of all other troops is to contribute their utmost to the success of the command of which the medical service is a part" (Army Field Manual FM 8-10, *Medical Service Theater of Operations*, March 1951, page 195). This field manual defines the medic's duties as follows:

The mission of the medical service in a theater of operations is to contribute to the success of the military effort through—

a. Conserving Manpower. Military strength is preserved by seeing that only the fit take the field, by the protection of troops against unnecessary hazards to health and efficiency, and by effective care and early return to duty.

b. Preventing Adverse Effects of Unevacuated Casualties on Combat Efficiency. Casualties within any combat unit restrict its movement. Lack of care and proper evacuation reduces the soldier's willingness to take necessary risks. Both can be prevented by adequate medical aid and rapid evacuation [page 20].

In trying to decide whether to apply for a I-A-O or I-O classification, therefore, you should consider what degree of cooperation with the military your beliefs will permit. Few

COs are unwilling to give medical assistance and other aid to injured and sick persons. But in deciding whether you can serve as an Army medic, you must consider not only the kind of service you will perform but the context and overall purpose as well. If your beliefs as a CO allow you to perform life-saving duties without regard to the fact that your services are regarded by the Army as a necessary part of its war-making function, you may find yourself satisfied with the I-A-O classification. If not, you will need to consider the I-O classification.

While you are performing military service as a I-A-O, you are classified I-C. After your service is completed, you are classified IV-A. You are not eligible to re-enlist in the armed forces, but you receive the same veterans' benefits as other ex-soldiers.

CIVILIAN ALTERNATE SERVICE: I-O, I-W

If your convictions do not allow you to serve in any military capacity, even as a noncombatant, you may be classified I-O by your draft board. This classification allows the board to assign you to a civilian alternate service job at the time other men your age are drafted into the Army. Perhaps because I-O registrants do not serve in the armed forces (and therefore do not help fill the local board's monthly quota), this classification is usually much harder to get than I-A-O. Even so, there are more I-Os than I-A-Os. About 2,000 I-A-Os per year complete the Army's non-combatant training program, while in the summer of 1968 more than 27,000 men were classified as I-O type conscientious objectors and over 6,000 were performing civilian alternate service (*Selective Service,* September 1968).

If you receive the I-O classification, you will be processed in the usual way. You are still eligible for any deferments (except I-S(C), discussed in Chapter 9), and can appeal a I-O classification like any other. You will be ordered to take an armed forces physical examination when you are close to being called for service, if you haven't already passed one. Unlike men in other classifications, as a I-O you may refuse to take the examination without being considered delinquent, but you will then be considered acceptable for civilian work [LBM 64]. If you believe you should be rejected for medical reasons, you may take the examination and follow the steps outlined in Chapter 13.

If you are classified I-O, the Regulations require that you submit to your local board a list of up to three types of work which you are able and willing to do. This is to be done "within ten days after a Statement of Acceptability (DD Form 62) has been mailed to [you] by the local board or within ten days after [you have] failed to report for or submit to armed forces physical examination" [REG 1660.20(a)]. In practice, the local board takes the initiative by sending you a Special Report for Class I-O Registrants (Form 152) [LBM 64].

However, it is not necessary to wait until you receive this form. If you wish to speed up the process, you can file an Application of Volunteer for Civilian Work (Form 151) at any time, before or after you have received a I-O classification. If you volunteer before you are classified I-O, the board must immediately consider your CO application [REG 1660.10]. Unfortunately, some boards, particularly in Minnesota, send Form 151 to all registrants who request Form 150, seeming to imply that a CO should be willing to give up any deferments he qualifies for and perform civilian work immediately, and giving the impression that those who don't volunteer may be assumed to be insincere. This sort of pressure is inconsistent with the idea of "volunteering" and the practice seems improper and perhaps illegal.

You will be required to spend two years in "civilian work contributing to the maintenance of the national health, safety, or interest" [MSSA 6(j)]. You can work for a government agency, federal, state, or local. You can also work for a nonprofit private organization, provided your work serves the public, not just the members of the organization [REG 1660.1]. You usually cannot work in your home community, though this is subject to definition in a highly mobile society, and in any case can be permitted at the local board's discretion [REG 1660.21(a)]. The national director advises that "the position should be one that cannot readily be filled from the available competitive labor force" [LBM 64], which often means only low-paying or unattractive jobs are approved. However, the instructions on Form 152 provide that "it will be the policy of the Selective Service System whenever possible to order you to civilian work which will most fully utilize your experience, education and training." It should be noted that the director's memorandum is only advisory, while Selective Service forms are part of the Regulations [REG 1606.51(a)].

Many boards insist that your civilian work assignment be chosen from the lists at local boards (the instructions to Series I of Form 152 reflect this practice). These lists include organizations which often employ COs and have general approval from the state or national director of Selective Service. However, in practice you may be allowed to perform suitable work not on these lists if you find a job and submit a letter from the employer offering to hire you for two years and explaining that the work and the organization meet the requirements for civilian alternate service. Since most of the jobs on the local board lists are in general hospitals, mental institutions, and old people's or children's homes, you may prefer to find your own job if your interests and abilities equip you for a different sort of work. In recent years, local

Form approved,
Budget Bureau No. 33–R127.

SELECTIVE SERVICE SYSTEM

APPLICATION OF VOLUNTEER FOR CIVILIAN WORK

(Stamp of local board at which application is
filed if other than local board of jurisdiction)

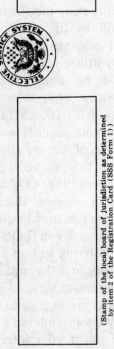

(Stamp of the local board of jurisdiction as determined
by item 2 of the Registration Card (SSS Form 1))

I hereby volunteer for civilian work contributing to the maintenance of the national health, safety, or interest and request that I be ordered to perform this work under the provisions of the Military Selective Service Act of 1967, and the rules and regulations prescribed thereunder. For this purpose, I waive all rights of personal appearance and appeal if I am classified as available for such civilian work, and I consent to my being ordered to perform this work at any time convenient to the Government.

My Selective Service number is

212

My Local Board is No. .... at ....
(City, town or county, State, and ZIP Code)

I was born ....
(Month) (Day) (Year)

My mailing address is ....
(Number and street or R.F.D. route)

....
(City, town, or village) (County) (State) (ZIP Code)

....
(Signature of registrant)

....
(Date of application)

Instructions: Prepare in duplicate, the original for filing in the Cover Sheet (SSS Form 101), the duplicate for delivery to the registrant.

SSS Form 151

U.S. GOVERNMENT PRINTING OFFICE : 1968—O-288-928

213

Form approved.
Budget Bureau No. 33–R128.

SELECTIVE SERVICE SYSTEM

SPECIAL REPORT FOR CLASS I–O REGISTRANTS

(Local Board Stamp)

Form to be returned on or before _____

Date of mailing _____

Date received back at local board _____

(Selective Service Number)

To _____
    (Last name)   (First name)   (Middle name)

Mailing address _____
    (Street and number)   (City, town, or village)   (State)   (ZIP Code)

To Class I–O Registrants:

A registrant placed in Class I–O who has received his Certificate of Acceptability (DD Form 62) or who failed to report for or submit to Armed Forces physical examination shall, in accordance with Selective Service Regulations prescribed by the President, be ordered by his local board to perform for a period of twenty-four (24) consecutive months such civilian work contributing to the maintenance of the national health, safety, or interest as the local board may deem appropriate.

The Selective Service Regulations require you to submit to your local board, within ten (10) days after a Certificate of Acceptability (DD Form 62) is mailed to you or within ten (10) days after you have failed to report for or submit to an Armed Forces physical examination, three (3) types of approved civilian work which you are qualified to perform and which you offer to perform in lieu of induction into the Armed Forces. A list of the types of approved civilian work is on file in local board offices. The types of work you offer to perform, your prior work experience, and your other pertinent qualifications should be set forth under the appropriate items of this form.

If you fail to submit to the local board the types of work which you offer to perform, or if the local board finds that none of the types of work submitted by you has been approved, or is appropriate, it will submit to you by letter three (3) types of approved work which it deems appropriate for you to perform. Within ten (10) days after such letter has been mailed to you by the local board, you shall file with the local board a written statement signifying acceptance or rejection of any or all of the types of work submitted. If any types are acceptable to you the local board will order you to perform one of the types of work which you have offered to perform. If you do not offer to perform any of the types of work submitted by the local board, a meeting will be held at a time and place of which you will be mailed notice and at which you will have an opportunity to reach an agreement with the local board as to the type of work which you will perform. If no agreement can be reached at such meeting the local board, after approval by the Director of Selective Service, will order you to perform such work as is deemed appropriate by the local board.

In no case will you be required to perform work until you have been mailed an Order to Report for Civilian Work and Statement of Employer (SSS Form 153). This order will allow you a minimum of ten (10) days after the date on which it is mailed to you to report for work. However, your local board will not order you to work prior to the time you would have been ordered to report for induction if you had not been classified in Class I-O unless you file with the local board an Application of Volunteer for Civilian Work (SSS Form 151) which establishes that you desire to be ordered to work as soon as possible without regard to your normal order of selection.

By submitting a choice of employment you have an opportunity to select the type of work you will be more interested in and perhaps best qualified to do. There may be opportunities for performing approved types of work with nonprofit organizations, associations, or corporations or with local, State, or Federal governmental agencies. If you are qualified for positions that require special skills, training, technical knowledge, or professional education and experience, you should list any additional information that will be of assistance to the employer in assigning you to work that can utilize your highest level of aptitude and skill.

In the event you have applied to one of the approved employers for work and have a definite answer to your application, you should show this in Series II on the form. The local board cannot secure special skilled positions for you. However, it will be the policy of the Selective Service System whenever possible to order you to civilian work which will most fully utilize your experience, education and training.

The Military Selective Service Act of 1967, provides that any person who knowingly fails or neglects to obey an order from his local board to perform civilian work, as required by section 6 (j) thereof, shall be deemed to have violated the provisions of the Military Selective Service Act of 1967, and shall be subject to the punishment provided by that act.

SSS Form 152

(Clerk, Executive Secretary, or member of the local board)

1

SERIES I—WORK QUALIFICATIONS

In accordance with Selective Service Regulations I am submitting in order of preference, three (3) types of approved civilian work, selected from a list on file at a selective service local board, which I am qualified to do and which I offer to perform in lieu of induction into the Armed Forces as follows:

1. FIRST TYPE:

_____

_____

2. SECOND TYPE:

_____

_____

3. THIRD TYPE:

SERIES II—APPLICATION FOR APPROVED EMPLOYMENT

If you have applied to an approved employer for civilian work contributing to the national health, safety, or interest, and he has accepted your application, indicate:

Name of employer --

Address of employer ---
(Number and street)   (City)   (State)   (ZIP Code)

Type of employment --

Remarks --

(Signature of registrant)

Fill out work experience record on opposite side.

2

217

SERIES III—IMPORTANT CIVILIAN WORK EXPERIENCE

1. Describe your longest and most important jobs— Begin with your most recent job

A. Name of Employer:

Name job and describe exactly what you did and how you did it:

Address

Employer's business

DATE JOB STARTED	DATE JOB ENDED	FINAL PAY PER WK.

B. Name of Employer:

Name job and describe exactly what you did and how you did it:

Address

Employer's business

DATE JOB STARTED	DATE JOB ENDED	FINAL PAY PER WK.

C. Name of Employer:

Name job and describe exactly what you did and how you did it:

Address

Employer's business

DATE JOB STARTED	DATE JOB ENDED	FINAL PAY PER WK.

D. Name of Employer:

Name job and describe exactly what you did and how you did it:

Address

Employer's business

DATE JOB STARTED	DATE JOB ENDED	FINAL PAY PER WK.

2. ABILITIES AND INTERESTS

218

SPECIAL SKILLS (Check those in which you have experience)

....Accounting	....Child Welfare	....Electricity	....Animal Husbandry
....Bookkeeping	....Handicrafts	....Mechanics	....Fruit Growing
....Filing	....Playground Supervision	....Plumbing	....Gardening
....Shorthand	....Group Singing	....Licensed Car Driver	....Cooking
....Typing	....Painting	....Licensed Truck Driver	....Sewing
....Nursing	....Masonry	....Dairying	....Laundry
....Teaching	....Carpentry	....Poultry Farming	....Other (Describe below)

Other ——

Describe training, experience, and degree of proficiency in the skills in which you are most interested. ————————

——

——

List any special hobbies or interests you may have ——

3. LANGUAGES, other than English (check appropriate space) S-speak; R-read; W-write:

	Spanish			French			German			Low German			Other ( ) ( )		
	S	R	W	S	R	W	S	R	W	S	R	W	S	R	W
Fairly well															
Fluently															

3

4. EDUCATION:

A. I have completed _____ years of elementary school, _____ years of junior high school, and _____ years of
                 (Number)   (Number)   (Number)
high school.

B. I _____ graduated from high school.
   (was, was not)

C. I have had the following schooling other than elementary and high school (if none, write "None"):

Name of College, University, Preparatory, Trade, or Business School	Course of Study	Length of Time Attended, Degrees or Certificates Granted

REGISTRANT'S CERTIFICATE

I, _____, certify that I am the registrant named and described in the fore-
going statements in this report; that I have read (or have had read to me) the statements made by and about me,
and that each and every such statement is true and complete to the best of my knowledge, information, and belief. The
statements made by me in the foregoing _____ in my own handwriting.
                                   (are, are not)

Registrant sign here ☞ _____
                                   (Signature or mark of registrant)

                                         Date _____

_____
(Signature of witness to mark of registrant)

THE REGISTRANT WILL MAKE NO ENTRIES IN THIS SPACE

The registrant identified above is found qualified for the following types of civilian work contributing to the national health, safety, or interest in the order shown:

1. _____

2. _____

3. _____

_____
(Signature of local board member or employer)

_____
(Title)

_____
(Date)

U.S. GOVERNMENT PRINTING OFFICE : 1968—O—292-143

4

boards have sometimes approved work in medical research, forestry, settlement houses, agricultural research, and work for state highway and sanitation departments, and occasionally even in VISTA, United Nations agencies, organizing and service in poverty programs, teaching, legal aid, and draft counseling. The Peace Corps cannot be approved, but similar programs of work overseas, sponsored by private and religious organizations, employ COs. It must be emphasized, however, that while a local board has almost absolute power to decide whether a particular job is "appropriate" [REG 1660.20], the national and state directors really make most of the decisions.

A few draft counseling services keep lists of job openings suitable for alternate service, and the CO Services section in the Philadelphia office of the American Friends Service Committee can help you find current job listings. For the more interesting jobs, however, you will probably have to rely on your own imagination, ingenuity, and contacts.

If the jobs you submit are rejected, the board must submit three choices it has made, and you will be assigned to one of these if you accept it. If you reject all three, you will be asked to attend a meeting of the local board with a representative of the state director who will "offer his assistance in reaching an agreement." If no agreement is reached, the local board will select a job, with the approval of the national director, and order you to perform it [REG 1660.20, LBM 14]. Although these four steps have time limits specified in the Regulations, in practice you will usually be given extra time to find a job or make arrangements with a prospective employer, if you are willing to cooperate by finding work which your local board is willing to approve.

When a job is selected, the local board will issue an Order to Report for Civilian Work and Statement of Employer

(Form 153). If you report, you will be classified I-W while you are doing civilian work.

You should receive the normal pay, vacation, and other benefits of your job while you are in civilian alternate service, and be treated just as other employees are. The employer may fire you, in which case the state director of Selective Service for the state where you are working must assign you to similar work elsewhere. However, you are not free to leave your job without the permission of the state or national director until your two years are over.

Under some circumstances, you may be allowed to transfer to a different employer, be given retroactive credit for work done before you were officially ordered to begin, or be released early from civilian work [REG 1660.21(c) and (d), LBM 64]. After you have completed the required time, you will be classified I-W(Rel.).

Work in civilian service as a I-W can be for some a way of demonstrating peaceful alternatives to war through social service. However, if you have difficulty in imagining any form of alternate service acceptable to a draft board which could satisfy your sense of religious or humanitarian vocation, or if you are conscientiously opposed to the draft law itself, you may find yourself troubled by the idea of conscripted service in the context of a military manpower system. Some men who could qualify as conscientious objectors but who were opposed on principle not only to military service but to any forced service, have rejected I-O status and refused to cooperate with the draft.

Form approved.
Budget Bureau No. 33-R0129

SELECTIVE SERVICE SYSTEM

ORDER TO REPORT FOR CIVILIAN WORK AND STATEMENT OF EMPLOYER

(LOCAL BOARD STAMP)

To _____
    (First name)   (Middle name)   (Last name)

Mailing address _____
    (Street and number)   (City)   (State)   (ZIP Code)

Having been found to be acceptable for civilian work contributing to the maintenance of the

national health, safety, or interest you have been assigned to _____
                                                                    (Type of work)

located at _____
            (Name and address of employer)

_____
(Date of mailing)

_____
(Selective Service Number)

You are ordered to report to the local board named above at _____.m. on the _____ day of
_____, 19____, where you will be given instructions to proceed to the place of employment.
(hour)

You are ordered to report for employment pursuant to the instructions of the local board, to remain in employment for twenty-four (24) consecutive months or until such time as you are released or transferred by proper authority.

You will be instructed as to your duties at the place of employment.

Failure to report at the hour and on the day named in this order, or to proceed to the place of employment pursuant to instructions, or to remain in this employment the specified time will constitute a violation of the Military Selective Service Act of 1967, which is punishable by fine or imprisonment or both.

_____
(Clerk, Executive Secretary, or Member of the Local Board)

STATEMENT OF EMPLOYER

The above registrant (check one) ☐ has ☐ had not reported for civilian work as of the date of this statement.

Name of Employer _____

Address of Employer _____
(Street address)   (City)   (State)   (ZIP Code)

_____
(Signature of employer or agent)

_____
(Title)

_____
(Date)

SSS Form 153   (Revised 6-5-67)   (See instructions on reverse side)

225

INSTRUCTIONS

An original and five copies of this form shall be prepared by the local board for each registrant ordered to report for civilian work contributing to the national health, safety or interest. The original shall be mailed to the registrant at least ten (10) days before the day set for him to report to the local board and a copy filed in his Cover Sheet (SSS Form 101). Four copies shall be mailed to the employer, one completed copy to be retained by the employer, three completed copies to be returned to the local board. The local board shall file one completed copy in the registrant's Cover Sheet (SSS Form 101), and forward two completed copies to the State Director of Selective Service, one to be retained for his use, the other to be forwarded to the Director of Selective Service.

When the registrant reports to the place of employment, the employer will complete the Statement of Employer and mail three copies to the local board of registration, shown in the box at the upper left hand corner of this form. If the registrant does not report within 48 hours after the date he is scheduled to arrive at the place of employment, the employer should immediately notify the registrant's local board by mail.

GPO 928-528

226

PART V

EMIGRATION

"Many of our forefathers came to this country to get out from under the burden of conscription in Europe. I have yet to hear these ancestors referred to as 'draft dodgers,' or the men now going to Canada referred to as 'Pilgrims.'"

ANONYMOUS

CHAPTER SIXTEEN

LEAVING TO AVOID THE DRAFT

What kinds of men emigrate because of the draft? The only safe generalization is that, more than most men, they do not want to be drafted, but have chosen not to confront it and accept the risk of prison. They have a variety of reasons. Many are non-political; although they may despise the draft, they are not prepared to commit civil disobedience aimed at influencing others, as are the resisters discussed in Chapter 18. Others are political but don't think going to prison will have an effect on public opinion worth their sacrifice. Still others have come to feel that America is not worth trying to change, or is so far gone as to be hopeless. Many fear the effect of prison on career, marriage, family relationships, or psychological condition. They are often attracted to a country like Canada because it seems a new, open frontier.

A large number of draft emigrants are motivated at least partly by opposition to the war in Vietnam. Some are opposed to that war but would participate in other wars, and therefore don't expect to be recognized as conscientious objectors (see Chapter 14). Others are opposed to all war and either were denied classification as COs, or oppose the draft entirely and will not accept CO status.

Those who emigrate are often well educated, usually with some college, often with one or more degrees. This is partly because it's easier to be admitted to most countries as a permanent resident if you have education and skills, and partly because fewer uneducated men think of opposing military service by leaving their native country.

Beyond this, it's almost impossible to generalize. Emigrants vary in philosophy from very conservative to revolutionary leftist to hippie, with heaviest representation between these extremes. They are ambitious and lazy, unkempt and neat, strange and ordinary, married and single, nervous and self-confident. What they have in common is a decision that they would rather start a new life in another country, knowing they will probably never be free to return to the United States, than serve in the armed forces or go to prison.

If you are going to leave because of the draft, it may be important to get answers to a number of questions. The most important of these is "Why?" The answer may seem obvious, but many of those who go find that it isn't. Some discover that their reasons for going weren't as strong as the attachments to home, family, and familiar way of life. Some feel they have deserted their friends at a time when they were needed, when it was essential to change America into a more just and peaceful country, and that they can have little influence on America's future from abroad. A number have decided to return and face arrest.

But they are in the minority. Most emigrants have not returned. Some are entirely happy in their new lives. Others aren't satisfied but would rather have their dissatisfaction than a prison term.

WHEN TO LEAVE

As long as you are going to a country that isn't interested in your draft status and won't deport or extradite you because of it (discussed below), it makes little difference legally when you leave. Thee are possible advantages (also discussed below) to going before the date you are supposed to report for induction, but in most cases these aren't important. You are still able to leave after refusing induction or failing to report. Probably the cutoff date is the day you are arrested for a draft offense. Leaving while you are on bail awaiting trial may present special problems, probably including loss of the bail and a more severe punishment if you ever return, and may make it harder for other men to get out on bail.

WHERE TO GO

You should, theoretically at least, be able to go to any country that meets three tests:

1. You find it an attractive place to live, and can earn a living there.
2. It won't extradite you for your draft violation.
3. You can get the right to live there permanently.

You will have to judge the first element for yourself on the basis of as much information as you can get, and preferably advance visits to see how well you will like the new country as a permanent home. You may want to consider whether you will be eligible for that country's draft, if it has one.

You must also consider the possibility of extradition, the legal process by which you may be turned over to American authorities to be tried for a crime of which the United States had accused you. Extradition is possible only for a crime listed in the treaties between the United States and the country you are in. There seem to be only a few countries whose extradition treaties with the United States include draft offenses, and all of these are in Latin America: Argentina, Chile, Colombia, the Dominican Republic, Ecuador, El Salvador, Guatemala, Honduras, Mexico, Nicaragua, and Panama. Despite the treaties, with the exception of Mexico, where there are reports of men being returned to the

United States by Mexican officials without any formal legal action, we have never heard of extradition from these countries actually taking place in draft cases.

Getting a visa as an immigrant or permanent resident may be a problem in some countries. Many Americans find England attractive because it is English-speaking, temperate in climate, culturally rich, and without a draft. But it is almost impossible to be admitted to England as an immigrant, so it is rarely an option.

Because of these three considerations, most draft emigrants choose Canada. Its extradition treaty does not include draft offenses. It is English-speaking, economically and culturally similar to the United States in many areas, and an attractive land with attractive people and a liberal government. It has no draft. And it is in need of more people with education and job skills, so it readily grants "landed immigrant" status to those who meet its standards. Chapter 17 is devoted to the details of emigration to Canada.

CAN YOU EVER RETURN?

It must be emphasized that the draft emigrant must choose a *permanent* home. If you leave the United States to avoid the draft, there is no certainty that you can ever return, even for a visit. There are two possible reasons for this, depending on whether you remain a U.S. citizen or renounce your citizenship.

If You Remain a U.S. Citizen

It is not illegal to move to another country, but you remain legally subject to the draft as long as you remain a U.S. citizen, regardless of where you live or whether you have legal status as a visitor, student, or immigrant there.

Therefore, your draft board will continue processing your file after you leave. If you fail to perform any duty—to notify it of your mailing address, to return questionnaires it sends to you, to take a pre-induction physical examination—you are likely to be declared delinquent and sent an induction order (see Chapter 7). Even if you perform these duties, you are likely, at the normal time, to be sent an induction order. If you don't submit to induction into the Army, or report for civilian work if you are classified as a I-O conscientious objector, you are almost certain to be reported for prosecution to the U.S. Attorney. A warrant for your arrest will in time be issued, and it will be waiting for you if you ever return to American territory. There is no time limit; it will be outstanding indefinitely. (There is a five-year statute of limitations for draft offenses, after which you can't be prosecuted, but it apparently applies only if you remain in the United States.)

Some emigrants hope that a general amnesty will eventually be declared for men who have left the United States because of the draft, perhaps after the Vietnam war is over. This would have the effect of canceling arrest warrants and leaving draft emigrants free to return without fear of arrest and prosecution. But the United States has no history of such amnesties, and this is at best a distant hope, dependent on future changes in U.S. policies and public opinion.

Without an amnesty, you can expect that a warrant will eventually be issued for your arrest and that you can thereafter return only if you decide to accept arrest and trial for your draft offense.

If You Give Up Your U.S. Citizenship

There are two ways to lose U.S. citizenship. The first is by becoming a citizen of another country, since the United

States no longer recognizes dual citizenship. However, this may take a long time—five years from the time you are admitted to Canada as a landed immigrant, for example. Violations of American laws committed while you were still a U.S. citizen will not be canceled by giving up that citizenship, and you will still be subject to arrest if you return to the United States even though you have become a citizen of another country.

However, it is possible to give up your U.S. citizenship even before you become a citizen of another country. You must go to a U.S. embassy or consultate in another country and go through the brief formality of "renouncing" your U.S. citizenship. The papers are filed with the U.S. State Department and you cease to be a U.S. citizen and are not subject to American laws.

If you move to another country and renounce your American citizenship before you have violated the draft law, you are not subject to arrest if you return. This means you should be sure that you have fulfilled all draft obligations—such as notifying your local board of your new address—up to the time you renounce your citizenship. Probably the last possible time to renounce citizenship to avoid prosecution would be just before the date you were supposed to report for induction or civilian work. When you notify your draft board that you are living abroad and have renounced your U.S. citizenship, it should probably reclassify you IV-C as an alien living outside the U.S. (see pages 161-162).

However, there are at least two serious disadvantages to renouncing citizenship.

First, there is no certainty that you could ever re-enter the United States. The U.S. must admit its citizens, but you would no longer be a U.S. citizen. If the U.S. government denied permission to visit, you might have no legal remedy. Whether officials at border crossing points will have lists of "unwelcome visitors" in the future, and whether they would include men who emigrated and renounced citizenship because of the draft, cannot now be determined. But since the only practical advantage of renouncing citizenship is keeping open the possibility of returning to the U.S. without being arrested, this possibility must be given serious thought.

Second, until you are admitted to citizenship in your new country, you are not a citizen of any country. You have no passport for travel outside your host country. And if you violate the conditions of your admission—in some cases this could be done by being arrested on a narcotics charge, by applying for public welfare, or by needing to be placed in a mental or tuberculosis institution—you would be entirely without a country; you would have no right to remain in the new country or return to the United States, and would have to go wherever you could be admitted. In some ways, being "stateless" is the worst of all conditions.

Furthermore, renunciation of your original citizenship may create problems when you apply for citizenship in the new country. It may even make you ineligible to stay as a visitor in some countries. For all of these reasons, very few draft-age Americans who emigrate to other countries renounce their U.S. citizenship, and most of the organizations in Canada and other countries that assist and advise draft emigrants recommend against it.

CURRENT INFORMATION

If you are planning to emigrate, it is advisable to visit the country in which you would live—and if possible the city—before making a final decision. You should look into living conditions, employment opportunities, and attitudes toward American draft emigrants. You should also talk with one of the organizations there that aid and advise draft emigrants; such committees exist in Canada and a number of European countries. Foreign embassies and consulates in the United States may have some information. It is important to have up-to-date information on immigration rules and practices, and advice on the best ways to proceed. The organizations that aid draft emigrants may also provide help in getting settled, finding work, and meeting new friends. Chapter 21 lists some sources of information about emigration.

CHAPTER SEVENTEEN

EMIGRATION TO CANADA

Since most Americans who leave the United States to avoid being drafted go to Canada, this chapter supplies information about the Canadian immigration laws which may affect you if you decide to go there.

It is not possible in this short chapter to provide full details. For full information, you will need to consult the Canadian organizations listed in Chapter 21. In addition, these practices, like all others discussed in this book, are always subject to change, so it is especially important that you be in touch with an organization in Canada which aids American draft emigrants before you make final plans. All we have tried to give in this chapter is a general picture to help you decide whether you are interested in emigrating to Canada and whether you are likely to be admitted.

Many Americans find Canada an attractive country. In most areas it is very like the United States in way of life, economy, culture, and speech, with an element of England added. In Quebec province and the other French-speaking areas, it resembles provincial France with American and English elements. There is conflict between the English- and French-speaking sections, resulting in movements toward separatism for the French-speaking areas. Canada's politics are generally liberal by American standards, with a government more like that of England than the U.S. Its climate and geography are varied. It is much more rural than the United States, and has far more unsettled frontier, though its cities are as cosmopolitan, as interesting, and sometimes as beset with problems as ours, including unemployment for the less skilled. It is geographically slightly larger than the United States, but has a population of only twenty million, so it is far less involved in the international conflicts that preoccupy most larger countries. Its economy is dominated by American-owned corporations, and its government generally cooperates with that of the United States, but it has an independence of spirit that makes it quite different from the client states of Latin America.

The government of Canada does not offer formal asylum to Americans escaping from the draft, but Canadian immigration laws do not exclude you because of your draft status. Since Canada has no draft, and seems unlikely to start one after its unhappy experience with the World War II draft, the extradition treaties between Canada and the United States do not include any crimes related to the draft and you would be considered for admission without regard to your draft status.

To be admitted to Canada, you must have two kinds of qualifications. First, you must not fall into a "prohibited class." Second, you must meet the requirements for one of three kinds of admission: visitor, student, or landed immigrant.

PROHIBITED CLASSES

If you fall into one of the "prohibited classes," you are not eligible for admission to Canada. In addition, if you enter legally but fall into a prohibited class during your first five years in Canada, you can be deported. After five years, even if you don't become a Canadian citizen, you can be deported only for offenses in the first two groups listed below, or for falsifying on your admission form. If you become a citizen, you can't be deported for any reason. These are the prohibited classes:

1. Subversives. This might include people who have ever been members or associates of organizations subversive to democratic government, or those believed on reasonable grounds to be likely "to engage in or advocate subversion" or likely "to engage in espionage, sabotage, or any other subversive activity directed against Canada or detrimental to the security of Canada." Clearly this is subject to interpretation, and in practice tends to be limited. For example, the Communist Party is legal in Canada.

2. Narcotics users. Use, or even a reasonable suspicion of use, of any narcotic, unless more than five years earlier, is grounds for exclusion. Marijuana is regarded as a narcotic.

3. Criminals. Conviction or confession of a crime involving "moral turpitude" makes one ineligible for admission. "Moral turpitude," though not defined in the law, probably includes only serious crimes. This might not be enforced if the sentence was completed more than five years earlier, or two years earlier if the immigrant was convicted before he was 21.

4. Other excluded persons. Also excluded are prostitutes, homosexuals, mentally or physically defective or seriously diseased persons, chronic alcoholics, and "persons who are . . . or are likely to become public charges."

Of course, if you fall into one of the categories that exclude you from Canada, it is quite likely that you would also be found unsuitable for military service in the United States. The main exceptions are criminal convictions (discussed in Chapter 13), involvement with marijuana, and receipt of public welfare.

REQUIREMENTS FOR ADMISSION

Visitors

Millions of Americans visit Canada every year. Admission is normally a quick, easy process—a few questions about where you were born, where you are going in Canada, and how long you plan to stay, and a customs inspection of your baggage. If your appearance is unconventional, if you don't have enough money for a visit ($10 a day is assumed necessary), or if you have much more baggage than a visit requires, you are likely to be questioned more closely.

You can stay in Canada as a visitor for a maximum of six months. You can't go to school unless you change to student admission status (which can be done from within Canada). You also can't work unless you get a special permit or change to landed immigrant status (which also can be done from within Canada).

Students

If you have a letter of admission to a Canadian school and evidence that you have enough money to live in Canada (cash, bankbooks, evidence of a scholarship, or a letter from your parents saying they will support you), you generally will have no difficulty being admitted. Student admission is for a year at a time and may be renewed as long as you continue your studies. Your wife can be admitted with you, but neither of you can work without special permission. If you decide to stay in Canada after graduation, you can apply for landed immigrant status from within Canada. You will be just as eligible for a student deferment from your American draft board while you are a full-time student at a Canadian college as you would be at an American college (see Chapter 9).

Landed Immigrants

Only in this category are you admitted permanently to Canada. You are eligible to work, travel, or study. (You will be given student status if you indicate your intention to study when you apply for admission, but if you enter as a landed immigrant and later decide to become a student, your status will not be affected.) You will have the same rights as Canadian citizens except the right to vote, to hold certain government jobs, and to receive a Canadian passport (but you can still travel on your American passport, and even get it renewed, as long as you remain a U.S. citizen). After five years, you can apply for Canadian citizenship, or can remain in Canada without becoming a citizen.

Under the Immigration Regulations which went into effect on October 1, 1967, you can apply for landed immigrant status in any of five ways:

1. At the border. This is the fastest way. Generally it is recommended if your qualifications are uncertain, because rejection is usually informal; you will usually be able to withdraw your application if you are told that it will not be approved, and you can apply again elsewhere without having your previous rejection on the record.

2. From within Canada. You can enter as a visitor or student, and once in Canada apply for permanent status (in the case of the student, after you have finished your studies). This way is recommended only if your qualifications are good and you don't mind being unable to work until your application is approved—unless you get a special permit which may not be easy to get. Approval may take a few weeks or a few months. If you are rejected, however, it may be

difficult or impossible to try again, and you will have to leave Canada. The advantage of applying from within Canada is that you are safe from arrest for a draft violation while you are in Canada and have some time to collect the documents for your application for landed immigrant status, or to reconsider your decision.

3. By nomination or sponsorship. If you have a close relative in Canada who will take financial responsibility for you, admission will usually be very easy. The application is then filed by your relative, who might be a husband or wife, fiancé or fiancée, parent, grandparent, child, brother or sister, aunt or uncle, nephew or niece. You may be in Canada (as a visitor or student) or outside Canada when the application is filed.

4. By mail from outside Canada. This may take a number of months, but if your qualifications are very good it is a relatively easy way to complete all your arrangements before you actually leave the U.S. It avoids the interview involved in most other forms of application, which may be a disadvantage if you can make a good impression, or an advantage if you are likely to become nervous and make a poor impression. Since you are expected to wait for a reply after you have mailed your application, you should not apply by mail if your draft status may force you to leave the U.S. quickly.

5. At a Canadian consulate. You can file your application and receive your interview at the Canadian consulates in many major U.S. cities. You may have to wait as long as if you applied by mail, but will have the advantage of the interview to impress the official with your personal qualities.

However you apply, you will be evaluated on the same basis. You must score 50 out of a possible 100 "assessment units" unless you are sponsored or nominated (in which case there are different and easier requirements.) The units are given for the following qualifications:

1. Education and vocational training—up to 20 units—one for each year of school, apprenticeship, or other training.

2. Personal assessment—up to 15 units—given by the immigration officer on the basis of his evaluation of your adaptability, motivation, initiative, and general suitability for successfully settling in Canada.

3. Occupational demand—up to 15 units—based on estimates by the Immigration Department of the need for workers in Canada in your occupational field.

4. Occupational skill—up to 10 units—based on your highest skill, regardless of what work you actually intend to do, from ten units for professionals to one for unskilled workers.

5. Age—up to 10 units—all ten if your age is between 18 and 35, minus one unit for every year over 35.

6. Arranged employment—10 units—given if you have a definite job offer in Canada with prospects of continuity—given only if you apply from outside Canada or at the border, not if you apply from within Canada.

7. Knowledge of English and French—up to 10 units—five each for fluent knowledge of English and French, fewer units if you are less fluent.

8. Relative—up to 5 units—five for a relative in the city

where you will live who will help you, three if the relative lives elsewhere in Canada.

9. Employment opportunities in the area of destination—up to 5 units—based on the need for workers in the part of Canada where you will live.

There are special rules if you are planning to start a business in Canada and show you have the money and ability to succeed, or if you plan to retire there.

The application form for landed immigrants asks about these and other qualifications, including the places where you have lived and worked, the amount of money you are taking in or will later transfer to Canada, any debts you have, your marital status and children, organizations you belong to, criminal convictions, and health. You will need a number of documents or notarized letters to prove your identity, citizenship, marriage, education and training, ownership of the assets you claim to have, and other facts depending on individual circumstances. If your application is approved, you will be required to submit a report of a thorough medical examination.

The unit system makes admission as a landed immigrant a fairly objective process, though the judgment of the immigration officer is involved in some items. If you earn at least 50 units, don't fall into a prohibited class, and demonstrate that you have enough money to support yourself until you have a job (at least several hundred dollars), you are almost certain to be admitted. Even with 50 units, if the immigration officer believes that your scores "do not reflect the particular applicant's chances of establishing himself in Canada," he may reject you, but he then must explain the reasons in writing and receive the approval of a superior officer. Such rejections are unusual.

Most draft emigrants should meet these standards with

little difficulty. Even if the immigration officer isn't impressed with you, you would receive 12 units for high school graduation and one for every year of college and graduate study, 10 for being under 35 years old, 5 for speaking English, and more depending on your occupational skills and plans. If you aren't sure you qualify, you may want to visit the city where you will live and try to get a firm job offer there (conditional, of course, on your being admitted); this will give you 10 extra units. Most major cities in Canada have committees to aid draft immigrants, and they can sometimes help find jobs.

There are often rumors that Canada is about to "close the border." These have always proven untrue. Even if the border is "closed," this will merely mean that you can't apply for landed immigrant status at the border. The other four ways, including entering as a visitor and applying from within Canada, would remain available.

PART VI

TRIAL AND PRISON

"Unjust laws exist: shall we be content to obey them, or shall we endeavor to amend them, and obey them until we have succeeded, or shall we transgress them at once? Men generally, under such a government as this, think that they ought to wait until they have persuaded the majority to alter them. They think that, if they should resist, the remedy would be worse than the evil . . . .

"If the injustice is part of the necessary friction of the machine of government, let it go, let it go: perchance it will wear smooth,—certainly the machine will wear out. If the injustice has a spring, or a pulley, or a rope, or a crank, exclusively for itself, then perhaps you may consider whether the remedy will not be worse than the evil; but if it is of such a nature that it requires you to be the agent of injustice to another, then, I say, break the law. Let your life be a counter friction to stop the machine. What I have to do is to see, at any rate, that I do not lend myself to the wrong which I condemn."

HENRY DAVID THOREAU, "CIVIL DISOBEDIENCE"
(1849)

CHAPTER EIGHTEEN

TWO KINDS OF PRISONER—THE NONCOOPERATOR AND THE UNSUCCESSFUL COOPERATOR

The "Penalties" section of the Selective Service law provides that ". . . any person who . . . evades or refuses registration or service in the armed forces . . . or who in any manner shall knowingly fail or refuse to perform any duty required of him under or in the execution of this title, or rules, regulations, or directions made pursuant to this title . . . shall, upon conviction in any district court of the United States of competent jurisdiction, be punished by imprisonment for not more than five years or a fine of not more than $10,000 or by both such fine and imprisonment . . ." [MSSA 12(a)].

Despite this severe penalty, thousands of men have refused to be inducted into the armed forces or refused other duties provided in the law. Nearly all have done so with full knowledge of the possible penalty. Many have been convicted and sentenced to prison.

Nearly all of those who are actually sent to prison for violations of the Selective Service law are acting out of a firm belief that they are doing the right thing. Their beliefs are so strong that they would rather risk prison than violate them. If you feel this way, this chapter and the two that follow may give you some idea of why a minority of draft-age men openly violate the Selective Service law. Chapter 19 describes what is likely to happen to you in court and what chance you have to win there. And, in case you lose, Chapter 20 tells a little about life in a federal prison and the after-effects.

Most men who are tried for Selective Service violations can

be divided into two groups. Those who are opposed to the draft law or the policies it supports, and on principle refuse to obey its requirements, may be called "noncooperators." Others obey the Selective Service law so long as they are put into the classifications they feel they can accept. They refuse to obey the law when they are denied those classifications and are ordered to report for induction or civilian alternate service, and may therefore be called "unsuccessful cooperators." This distinction is convenient for discussion, but in fact many men fall somewhere between cooperators and noncooperators.

NONCOOPERATORS

There have always been a small number of men with strong objections to the draft. The number has increased greatly during the past few years as draft calls have risen because of the unpopular war in Vietnam. Those who refuse to cooperate express a wide variety of reasons for their actions.

Over the twenty years that America has had a "peacetime" draft, most noncooperators have acted out of a feeling that they are opposed to more than their own participation in war or military service. Therefore, they are unwilling to enter either civilian or noncombatant service when ordered by their draft boards.

Some act from strong opposition to the military. Although Selective Service is technically a civilian agency, its principal function is of course to provide men for the armed forces. Accepting its legitimacy, even by asking for a CO classification and doing work approved by the draft board, seems to some men an acceptance of the right of draft boards to order other men into the Army. Those who take this position feel that no man should be required to serve in the armed forces.

To them, cooperating with draft boards is no different from cooperating with the armed forces.

In other cases, noncooperators believe that the draft itself is an unacceptable system. They consider it an effort by the government to control and regiment the individual citizen. They resent having to register and keep their boards informed of their addresses and of any actions that could affect their classifications. They reject the idea that a group of people in the community—usually much older but not necessarily wiser than they—have a right to decide on behalf of the government whether they should be allowed to go to school, to work, or to live with their families. They will not willingly give up the right to control their own lives, even to an official government agency, and see this attempt to limit their freedom as illegitimate and dictatorial. They sometimes argue that the Thirteenth Amendment to the Constitution, which forbids "involuntary servitude," should make the draft illegal.

Many of today's noncooperators are responding particularly to the Vietnam war. They believe that men are being drafted to fight in a war which is immoral or illegal. They often point out that the Nuremberg trials of Nazi leaders after World War II were based on the principle that men are responsible for war crimes even if they were simply obeying the laws of their country or the orders given by their superiors. To them, the United States is involved in a war of aggression and is violating treaty obligations as well as international law.

As defined here, noncooperation is essentially an individual act, whether phrased in terms of conscience, religious belief, or political or social philosophy.

However, today more and more noncooperators feel that this is not enough. They wish not only to act justly themselves (as they view it) but also to influence others. They feel an obligation to make their acts politically and socially relevant, to attempt to bring their views to the attention not only of the government but of the people. Those who take this view usually call themselves draft resisters.

The resister is likely to try to make his position as public as possible. By publishing advertisements, holding meetings and demonstrations, being interviewed by newspaper and television reporters, distributing leaflets, and talking with as many others as possible, the draft resister tries to organize a strong enough movement to influence public opinion, stall the machinery of war, and in time affect the course of history.

Probably most of those who join the resistance groups which have sprung up since 1967 in nearly every large city and on many college campuses are primarily opposed to the war in Vietnam. But many are opposed to all war, to the draft, and to the conditions and social institutions which produce war and injustice.

There are almost as many resistance philosophies as there are resistance groups, but they seem to be variations of two essential attitudes. Probably best known to newspaper readers is the view that resisters should use their own public acts of civil disobedience, often including destroying draft cards or returning them to the government, as an organizing instrument to make their views known to others who feel the same way, and at the same time to challenge government policy. Less known, but perhaps more widely held, is the view that resisters should avoid breaking the law as long as possible to work toward organizing for basic social change, but refuse to be drafted if they finally receive induction orders.

Viewed as a form of protest, draft resistance clearly has

been effective in calling attention to the resisters' position. The price of this attention, of course, has been the alienation of many people who might agree with, or at least respect, the anti-war position but are repelled by the illegal and spectacular acts, and as a result regard even the most principled and disciplined resisters as anti-social and irresponsibly rebellious. However, their views would be much easier to ignore if they stayed strictly within the law. Press attention to the resistance movement has resulted from the dramatic and illegal nature of some of its actions—especially the burning and returning of draft cards and the destruction of Selective Service files.

A collection of statements by noncooperators and other war objectors, explaining why they took their various stands, appears in *We Won't Go,* edited by Alice Lynd (Beacon Press, 1968).

UNSUCCESSFUL COOPERATORS

By far the largest number of those who violate the Selective Service law don't define themselves as noncooperators. However they may feel about war, the draft, or Vietnam, they are willing to obey the law if they are given the status they think they are entitled to. If they violate the law, it is because they don't believe they have been properly classified by Selective Service.

A great many of those who refuse to accept military service or civilian alternate service are members of the Watchtower Bible and Tract Society, usually called Jehovah's Witnesses, who ask to be classified IV-D as ministers but are turned down. This group regards all of its members as ministers, responsible for teaching, speaking, and distributing literature, but on principle none of them are paid for their work as ministers and missionaries. As a result, most of them work to support their families and use their free time for ministerial duties. Their claims for IV-D classification are therefore usually rejected (see page 155) and they are generally offered the I-O classification as conscientious objectors. Some accept and perform civilian alternate service, but many refuse to accept any classification except IV-D because they believe their responsibilities to serve as ministers spreading God's word in the world must come before any service demanded by the government. More Jehovah's Witnesses go to prison for draft refusal than members of any other group.

Perhaps the second largest group in prison consists of members of the Religion of Islam (often called Black Muslims), who are conscientious objectors to the war in Vietnam and perhaps all war. Since most make no effort to obtain CO status from Selective Service, when they refuse induction there is virtually no legal defense available.

A small number of unsuccessful cooperators are men who filed claims as conscientious objectors but were turned down and refused to be inducted into military service. Before 1965 a number of CO applicants were rejected because their claims weren't based on what Selective Service considered "religious training and belief," but the broad definition of the Seeger decision (see Chapter 14) has virtually eliminated court convictions in these cases. Today most convictions of unsuccessful CO claimants occur because the applicant doesn't provide evidence to support his claim, doesn't use his appeal rights, or waits until a crisis develops before making his claim, thus calling his sincerity into question. Since the courts have very limited power to review the decisions made by draft boards (see Chapter 19), rejection for "insincerity" may be hard to challenge in court. Even so, most of those who go to prison lose at their trials by failing to use all possible Selective Service appeal rights before refusing induction. Nearly all of those who are persistent and careful in trying to gain recognition within the Selective Service System are eventually successful in either being recognized as COs or receiving some other status acceptable to them. Nonetheless, every year a small number of unsuccessful CO applicants, despite careful efforts to have their claims recognized, end up in court. It is men in this group who have a reasonable chance of being acquitted.

CHAPTER NINETEEN

LEGAL DEFENSE AND SENTENCES

If you provide as much evidence as possible for the classification for which you feel you qualify, use all your procedural rights, and persist in your claim, the chances are very good that Selective Service will recognize it. If not, your final chance may be the courts. A successful effort to make Selective Service obey the law may not only help you, but may establish principles that will protect the rights of others as well.

Your day in court requires a good attorney, one who knows not only the general principles of law but also the special and unusual problems involved in draft cases. If you expect to carry your case to the courts, you should choose an attorney and get his advice early in the process—if possible, as soon as it appears you will end up in court. If you are unable to pay for legal help, you are entitled to a court-appointed attorney. In a few cities they are appointed from panels of attorneys especially interested in and informed about Selective Service law, but otherwise court-appointed attorneys are often unfamiliar with Selective Service law and should be encouraged to contact the Central Committee for Conscientious Objectors or another counseling service. If you can afford legal fees, the organizations listed in Chapter 21 can help you find a competent attorney.

There are three ways you may obtain judicial review of the decisions of Selective Service. By far the most common is a criminal defense—defending yourself in court from a charge of breaking the law, often by refusing induction. The second is a "petition for a writ of habeas corpus"—allowing yourself to be inducted but immediately asking the court to release you from the armed forces on the grounds that your induction order was illegal. The third is an injunction—a court order stopping the induction order before you have obeyed or disobeyed it. This is complicated, and usually—but not always—unsuccessful.

If you refuse induction—or refuse an order to perform civilian work as a conscientious objector, or some other requirement of the draft law—you can expect to be arrested, usually within a few months, and tried in the Federal District Court where you refused induction or where you were ordered to work. If you plead "not guilty," you are not necessarily denying that you refused induction. More often, you are saying that your induction order was illegally issued by your draft board, and therefore that no crime was committed when you disobeyed it. If the court accepts your argument, you will be found not guilty and the indictment will be dismissed. Your file will be sent back to Selective Service to reconsider. If, however, the court disagrees and rules that your induction order was legally issued, you will be found guilty of violating the Selective Service Act. A prison sentence is then a real possibility, though not the only possibility.

You may prefer a less usual method if you are more willing to risk two years in the military than a term of imprisonment. You can accept induction into the Army, but make arrangements in advance with an attorney to file papers immediately requesting a court order—called a "writ of habeas corpus"—releasing you from military custody. You would use the same legal arguments in this case as you would use to defend yourself if you refused induction. You can file a habeas corpus action at any time, but its chances of success are greater if filed as quickly as possible. If the court agrees with your arguments, you will be ordered released from the armed forces. If your argument fails, you will remain a soldier. Therefore, if you believe your conscience will not allow you to obey military orders, you may find this a less satisfactory way to get a court review. If you remain in the armed forces but refuse to obey orders, you are likely to face court-martial, with fewer rights than civilian courts allow and often punishment under worse conditions.

Injunctive action is an effort to convince a court in advance that any induction order that might be issued to you under the circumstances would be unlawful, and that induction would result in substantial damage to you. The 1967 Selective Service Act attempts to prevent injunctive action, but the courts are divided at this writing on whether that part of the law is constitutional.

Federal courts have traditionally been greatly influenced by past decisions, called precedents, especially those of the U.S. Courts of Appeal and the Supreme Court. Today, however, this is less true than at any time in the past. Federal judges feel less bound by decisions made during World War II and before. This may be partially because the courts seem to be getting more sophisticated, more aware of the realities of modern life; partially because today there isn't the spirit of national unity which in all-out war causes courts to overlook all but the most glaring violations of individual rights by the government; and partially because strained relations between Congress and the courts, and between the Justice Department and Selective Service, have encouraged the courts to give closer attention to procedural errors by Selective Service. As a result, new principles are being developed by courts, and some of the information in this and other chapters may be outdated by the latest court decisions before you read this book.

Under present court decisions, what can cause an induction

order to be found unlawful? No matter which of the three methods you use to get a court review, the causes discussed here apply.

Although they overlap, the causes can be divided into four main categories: (1) procedural errors, (2) the lack of a factual basis for your draft board's classification, (3) the violation of rights guaranteed by the Constitution, and (4) conflict between the Regulations issued by the President and the Act passed by Congress.

Working backwards, let us take the fourth category first. Suppose you don't realize that you are a conscientious objector until after you receive an induction order. The Regulations don't allow reopening a classification after issuance of an induction order unless you undergo a change in status beyond your control [REG 1625.2]. Is your newly crystallized belief beyond your control? And what of the unconditional language of the law itself: "Nothing contained in this title shall be construed to require . . ." [MSSA 6(j)]? Some courts say that the Regulation cannot restrict the provision of the Act (*U.S. v. Underwood,* 151 F.Supp. 874, 1955; *U.S. v. Gearey,* 368 F.2d 144, 1966). Others (for example, *Keene v. U.S.,* 266 F.2d 378, 1959) accept the validity of the Regulation.

As another example of possible conflict between the Act and the Regulations, the courts have recently become interested in the Regulation which allows a draft board to declare you delinquent and take away any deferment you have (discussed in Chapter 7). Congress, in the law, set up certain deferments and exemptions, such as I-S, II-S, IV-A, and IV-D. If you meet all the requirements for one of these classifications and you return your draft cards, can your deferred or exempt classification be taken away by a "punitive reclassification" process set up by the Regulations but not authorized in the law? Selective Service says any deferment or exemption can be taken away if you are declared delinquent; the Department of Justice says some can and some can't; defense attorneys and at least one court (*Kimball v. S.S. Local Board No. 15*, S.D.N.Y., April 1968, 1 SSLR 3058) say that as long as you continue to qualify for a deferment you are not subject to punitive reclassification. At this writing, the question is scheduled for decision by the Supreme Court in *Oestereich v. S.S. Local Board No. 11.*

The third category, more frequently used as a defense, is to argue that the draft law, or some parts of the law or Regulations—at least as applied to a given case—are unconstitutional. Failures so far are: (1) Conscription without a declaration of war is unconstitutional; (2) The war in Vietnam is illegal and therefore drafting men to fight in it is unconstitutional (no court has yet admitted this argument into evidence); and (3) Any draft is a violation of the Thirteenth Amendment to the Constitution forbidding involuntary servitude.

A frequent Constitutional defense is that the action of Selective Service has been arbitrary and capricious, and therefore violates the "due process" requirements of the Fifth Amendment to the Constitution. This Constitutional defense thus leads into the second category of court arguments, that there was no factual basis for the classification. The courts have ruled that a draft board must have some reason, or rational "basis in fact," for the classification it gave and for the denial of the classification requested (*Estep v. U.S.*, 327 U.S. 114, 1946; *Dickinson v. U.S.*, 346 U.S. 389, 1953). In other words, your draft board can't legally refuse to give you a CO classification or a deferment for which you qualify unless there is information in your file that indicates you may not qualify for it. However, this allows a very limited review by the courts. The judge will not determine whether the draft board made a good decision; if he finds *any* facts in your file which support the board's action, he will refuse to overturn it. If the file has *no* evidence supporting the board's action, that action will be ruled arbitrary and therefore illegal.

The first category of argument listed, procedural error, is also related to the Constitutional "due process" argument. If a procedural error is found, and it is shown that it took away a right of value to you, the judge is very likely to rule in your favor. This is probably the argument most frequently successful in Selective Service cases. Large numbers of decisions lead to this conclusion: If Selective Service does not treat your fairly, the courts may very well take your side.

But a word of caution must be offered. The courts will ordinarily not consider any argument you offer unless you "exhaust the administrative remedies" before coming to court. This means you must try to use every Selective Service procedure that could result in your not being drafted. You must use all appeal rights, and must report for induction and take the final physical examination before refusing to step forward and be inducted, if you hope to defend yourself successfully in court by arguing that the induction order was illegally issued.

SENTENCES

Let us turn away from those who accept induction and take habeas corpus action, and from those who win in court, toward the plight of those who are found guilty of breaking the Selective Service Act. What are the consequences?

Perhaps the best that can happen is probation or a suspended sentence, which in practice are much the same thing. You would be under the supervision of a probation officer for up to five years, and may need his permission to marry, change jobs, or leave the federal court district where you live and work, and are obliged to report to him regularly. Their strictness varies greatly. If you broke the law for conscientious reasons, the judge will likely insist that your work be "in the national interest," similar to civilian alternate service (discussed in Chapter 15). If you violate the conditions, you can be sent to prison for the length of time of your initial suspended sentence or the length of your probation, or you can be resentenced by the same judge who gave you the first sentence.

If you are sentenced under the Youth Corrections Act, the maximum sentence is four years imprisonment and two years parole, which is like probation. After its completion, your conviction is "erased" and you have no criminal record.

The maximum sentence is five years imprisonment and a $10,000 fine. The national average sentence currently is about 33 months. Fines are seldom imposed. The most severe sentences during the government's last reported fiscal year, 1967, were given out by Oklahoma judges, who gave 10 out of 11 men five-year sentences. Throughout the country, 58 maximum sentences were given, while judges in 23 states placed 78 men on probation during the same period. That year, 248 men either had indictments dismissed, or were found not guilty in court.

Some lawyers are convinced that, in practice, the likelihood of a successful defense or favorable sentence depends more on the attitudes of the judge than the legal merits of your position.

CHAPTER TWENTY

PRISON AND AFTER

The growth in the number of conscientious objectors and draft resisters inevitably means more young men are spending up to five years in one of the 32 institutions run by the Federal Bureau of Prisons.

After a six-year period during which the total number of federal prisoners steadily declined, the total rose in 1968 to 20,250 prisoners, and the average age dropped one year. The director of the Bureau of Prisons does not offer an explanation, but the cause was probably the draft. The Bureau's official report for the fiscal year 1967 showed 604 Selective Service violators were received from the courts, compared with 266 the year before.

Jehovah's Witnesses (see Chapter 18) make up the largest single group of draft violators in prison at any given time; currently there are several hundred. Draft resisters, Muslims, and unsuccessful CO claimants make up most of the remainder.

Those who are merely trying to avoid military service, but are not motivated by any strong principle, seldom go to prison. They usually accept an opportunity to "volunteer" for the Army when they are caught. Only if the Army doesn't want them—for example because of a criminal record—do they sometimes end up in prison.

Selective Service violators can be found in about 18 of the 32 federal institutions. The most used of these are the Federal Prison Camp, Allenwood, Pennsylvania (minimum security); the Federal Correctional Institution, Sandstone,

Minnesota (medium security); the Medical Center for Federal Prisoners, Springfield, Missouri (in medium-security dormitories for able-bodied men, to help run the institution); the Federal Reformatory, Lompoc, California (for young adults); and the Federal Prison Camp, Safford, Arizona (minimum security). With rare exceptions, draft violators are not put in penitentiaries, which are maximum-security prisons, but they sometimes serve their sentences on medium-security prison farms attached to penitentiaries.

Each institution is different, in part because the wardens have leeway in deciding the visiting hours, the educational and recreational programs, censorship, and other administrative matters.

A few months or years in prison is not a fate worse than death, if only because it has a court-determined time limit.

The first hint, therefore, if prison is in your future, is to think in terms of going *through* prison, rather than *to* prison. It is not an end to your dreams but, at very worst, a nightmare from which you will eventually awaken.

It need not be that bad. To a substantial degree, it will be up to you. Your fellow prisoners will not be successful criminals or they would not be in prison. Most will not be professionals, which in part explains their getting caught. Often the same inadequacies which drive one man to drink cause another to commit an occasional crime. If you have a concern for others and orient yourself to their problems, you may have an exhausting but rewarding time in prison.

Men in prison are often considered social discards, and draft violators must accept the same label. Often, however, they have inner resources not available to the average inmate, and these will intrigue other inmates and ought to be shared. Perhaps nothing is more rewarding than sharing resources which will be increased, rather than diminished, in the process.

The second hint on "doing time" in a manner that will add to your wisdom is to use your initiative. Don't do only what you are told to do, or your decision-making powers may be impaired for weeks or months after release, or even permanently. Concentrate on areas where there are choices, and create choices.

Offer to teach a class in something you know a good bit about, whether it has wide appeal or not. See if you can set up a drama, poetry, or music group. Organize sports competitions or a prison newspaper. Involve as many other inmates as possible. Not only does success benefit many others, but even an unsuccessful attempt can create a sense of shared purpose and common effort. And time will slip by. Seek undeveloped talents in those around you. Take correspondence courses, which can be arranged, and encourage others to do so. See if the chaplain would sponsor discussion groups.

A prison experience is always difficult, but it can be a source of growth and even satisfaction if it comes about as a result of doing what to you is the right thing. Even in a totalitarian society, as each prison is, interesting and worthwhile things can be done.

The last hint is of a different nature. Many of the stories one hears about homosexual activity in jails and prisons are true. But forced sexual activity is less common in federal prisons than in city and county jails and state prisons. It is true that virtually any draft-age prisoner will be "propositioned" repeatedly, but physical assaults are rare. The vast majority of men, in prison or out, have a strong preference for willing sex partners, even though they may use aggressive methods to determine whether someone who appeals to them might be willing if they "play their cards right." If you are able to convey an active dislike for the prospect of a sexual relationship with another prisoner, you can be reasonably certain his threats of attack will remain verbal. Perhaps that is the most one can ask of a sexually starved artificial community. Certainly the armed forces have similar problems.

In any event, virtually no one serves the entire sentence given him by the judge. You become eligible for parole after serving one-third of your sentence, though it isn't usually granted the first time you are eligible. Under ordinary circumstances, you can count on being released after serving about two-thirds of your sentence, because of what is called "good time." If you receive a five-year sentence—which would be unusually long, since the national average is now about 33 months—you will ordinarily spend three years in prison even if you don't make parole. In general, the longer your sentence, the more likely you are to make parole.

Just as veterans enjoy special status in our society, with permanent advantages over non-veterans, so the man who goes to prison for a felony suffers permanent disadvantages. Ex-felons cannot vote or hold elective office in many states, nor work for the state government. Only California seems to distinguish between conventional ex-felons and those whose crimes were caused by their beliefs. In that state the latter can now vote, after many years of being disfranchised. Some state laws go further and make it difficult or even impossible to obtain the licenses necessary for certain kinds of work. Doctors and lawyers will have an unusually difficult time pursuing their professions. Practices vary depending on state laws, so it is impossible to generalize adequately.

Jobs requiring security clearance, with the federal government directly or with firms holding certain defense contracts, are likely to be closed to convicted draft violators, and even recognized COs for that matter. Ordinarily, however, these men are not interested in jobs requiring security clearance.

We know of no case where a draft violator was denied a

Presidential pardon on request, when the applicant was no longer of draft age. Such a pardon, requested on special forms addressed to the United States Pardon Attorney, removes all the restrictions discussed above.

As indicated in the previous chapter, if you are sentenced under the Youth Corrections Act you do not face the employment problems of convicted felons.

Who can predict whether the next generation will ask, "Dad, what did you do to stop the spread of communism in Southeast Asia?" or "Dad, what did you do to stop the war in Vietnam?" Prison, and its aftermath, is bearable if it comes as a result of following your conscience. If you are in doubt, veer toward the majority. And whether in doubt or not, try to be mature enough to accept the consequences.

PART VII

OTHER SOURCES OF AID

"Every person shall be deemed to have notice of the requirements of the Military Selective Service Act of 1967, upon publication by the President of a proclamation or other public notice fixing a time for any registration. This provision shall apply not only to registrants but to all other persons."

[REG 1641.1]

CHAPTER TWENTY-ONE

DRAFT COUNSELING AND LEGAL AID

NATIONAL COUNSELING ORGANIZATIONS

1. Central Committee for Conscientious Objectors (CCCO)
   National office: 2016 Walnut Street, Philadelphia, Pennsylvania 19103
   West Coast office: 437 Market Street, San Francisco, California 94105
   Midwest Office: Midwest Committee for Draft Counseling (MCDC), 179 N. Michigan Avenue, Chicago, Illinois 60601

Provides counseling in person and by mail on all draft matters; trains draft counselors; refers to local draft counselors and to attorneys; publishes *Handbook for Conscientious Objectors* ($1.00) and memorandums on deferments and legal problems; publishes bi-monthly *News Notes* (free).

2. National Service Board for Religious Objectors (NSBRO)
   550 Washington Building, 15th Street and New York Avenue, N.W., Washington, D.C. 20005

Counsels in person and by mail, specializing in church-oriented COs; assists COs in communicating with Selective Service National Headquarters; publishes *Statements of Religious Bodies on the Conscientious Objector* (50¢) and various memorandums.

3. American Friends Service Committee (AFSC), CO Services Section
   160 N. 15th Street, Philadelphia, Pennsylvania 19102

National headquarters of a Quaker organization with offices in many cities (listed below under city names if known to provide draft counseling). Provides counseling; refers to local counselors; distributes literature on the draft from many sources; maintains lists of civilian alternate service jobs for COs.

In addition to these, many religious organizations provide aid with draft matters, primarily to men applying as COs, and most peace and pacifist organizations offer counseling.

NATIONAL LEGAL ASSISTANCE ORGANIZATIONS

1. American Civil Liberties Union (ACLU)
   156 Fifth Avenue, New York, New York 10010

National office of an organization with local and state branches in most parts of the U.S. Local offices can usually recommend sources of legal aid, and both state and national offices handle a limited number of test cases on Constitutional issues at their own expense.

2. National Lawyers Guild (NLG)
   Box 673, Berkeley, California 94701

Publications office of a lawyers' association with chapters in several major cities. Can often refer to attorneys or attorneys' panels.

3. National Emergency Civil Liberties Committee (NECLC)
   421 Seventh Avenue, New York, New York 10001

Can refer to lawyers; takes some test cases at own expense.

In addition, there are attorneys' panels formed or in formation in a number of cities to give legal assistance in draft cases, often with provision for fees based on ability to pay. Draft counselors and counseling services can often suggest experienced lawyers in their areas.

CANADIAN COUNSELING ORGANIZATIONS

1. Toronto Anti-Draft Programme
   2279 Yonge Street, Toronto 12, Ontario, Canada
   Publishes *Manual for Draft-Age Immigrants to Canada* ($2.00)

2. Vancouver Committee to Aid American War Resisters
   P. O. Box 4231, Vancouver 9, British Columbia, Canada

3. Montreal Council to Aid War Resisters
   P. O. Box 231, Westmount 6, Montreal, Quebec, Canada

These three organizations are the largest, and generally the best informed, of more than 20 groups in Canadian cities which aid American draft emigrants. They can refer to the others, which provide more limited legal advice, information about local conditions, and aid in settling and finding work.

LOCAL COUNSELORS AND COUNSELING SERVICES

The list below is not intended to be complete. Some areas have many excellent counseling services, and the one or two listed organizations should be able to refer you to local services. Other areas have no counseling services of which we are aware. It is not possible for us to endorse the quality of all listed counseling services, since we are unable to stay currently informed about them. You will have to do your own evaluation, as suggested in Chapter 1.

Northeast

Concord, New Hampshire: Concord Peace Center, Pleasant Street

Nashua, New Hampshire: Nashua Draft Information Center, 16 Pine Street

Brookline, Massachusetts: Brookline Draft Counseling Service, 173 Davis Avenue

Cambridge, Massachusetts:
Draft Information Service, 5 Longfellow Park
Boston Draft Resistance Group, 102 Columbia Street

Worcester, Massachusetts: Worcester Draft Information Center, 340 Main Street, Room 362

Amherst, Massachusetts: Valley Peace Center, 2 Cook Place

West Hartford, Connecticut: American Friends Service Committee, 144 S. Quaker Lane

New Haven, Connecticut: Draft Action Group, 241 Orange Street

Great Neck, New York: Long Island Draft Information and Counseling Service, P. O. Box 125

Brooklyn, New York: Brooklyn Draft Information and Counseling Service, 53 Prospect Park West

New York, New York: American Friends Service Committee, 15 Rutherford Place

Bronx, New York: Bronx Draft Information and Counseling Service, 2409 Lorrilard

Scarsdale, New York: Westchester Draft Information and Counseling Service, Box 42, Heathcote Station

Albany, New York: Capitol Area Peace Center, 727 Madison Avenue

Binghamton, New York: Broome County Peace Center, 73 State Street

Ithaca, New York: Cornell Draft Information Service, 316 Anabel Talor Hall, Cornell University

Syracuse, New York: David Easter, 1513 E. Genesee Street

Rochester, New York: Rochester Resistance Draft Counseling Center, 116 St. Paul Street

Princeton, New Jersey: Draft Information Center, 173 Nassau Street.

Pittsburgh, Pennsylvania: Draft Information Center, Fifth & Bellefield Avenues

South

Richmond, Virginia: Southern Student Organizing Committee, 509 N. Ryland

Durham, North Carolina: Southern Student Organizing Committee, 1111 W. Chapel Hill Street

High Point, North Carolina: American Friends Service Committee, 1818 S. Main Street

Charlotte, North Carolina: Charlotte Draft Counselors, 2038 Randolph Road

Atlanta, Georgia:
American Friends Service Committee, 41 Exchange Place, S.E.
Atlanta Workshop in Nonviolence, 1036 Peachtree Street

Miami, Florida: AFSC Peace Center of Miami, 3356 Virginia Street, Room 202

Jackson, Mississippi: A. D. Beittel, 1666 Lelia Drive

Nashville, Tennessee: Southern Student Organizing Committee, 1703 Portland Avenue

Midwest

Cleveland, Ohio: Cleveland Draft Counseling Association, 11205 Euclid

Dayton, Ohio: American Friends Service Committee, 915 Salem Avenue

Cincinnati, Ohio: Cincinnati Draft Project, 4 W. 7th Street

Detroit, Michigan: Detroit Draft Counseling Service, Central Methodist Church, 23 E. Adams

Ann Arbor, Michigan:
  Ann Arbor Draft Counseling Center, 502 E. Huron
  American Friends Service Committee, 1222 Woodlawn
East Lansing, Michigan: East Lansing Draft Information
  Center, 911 E. Grand River
Indianapolis, Indiana: Indianapolis Draft Project, 222 E. 16th
  Street
Chicago, Illinois: American Friends Service Committee, 407
  S. Dearborn Street
DeKalb, Illinois: DeKalb Association for Draft Counseling,
  633 W. Locust
Milwaukee, Wisconsin:
  American Friends Service Committee, 3529 N. 3rd Street
  Milwaukee Organizing Committee, 3052 N. Stowell
Madison, Wisconsin: American Friends Service Committee,
  317 N. Brooks
Minneapolis, Minnesota:
  Twin Cities Draft Information Center, 1905 Third Avenue
    South, Room 201
  American Friends Service Committee, 807 Fourth Street,
    S.E.
Des Moines, Iowa: American Friends Service Committee,
  4211 Grand Avenue
Iowa City, Iowa: Iowa City Resist, 123½ S. Clinton
St. Louis, Missouri: Peace Information Center, 6244 Delmar
  Boulevard
Kansas City, Missouri: Peace Information Center, 306 W.
  39th Street
Wichita, Kansas: Draft Counseling Committee, Box 291

Southwest and West

Tulsa, Oklahoma: Tulsa Draft Counseling Center, 2330 N.
  Quaker

Houston, Texas: American Friends Service Committee, 4717 Crawford Street

Austin, Texas: Austin Draft Information Center, 700 Guadelupe

Denver, Colorado: American Friends Service Committee, 1460 Pennsylvania

Tucson, Arizona: Tucson Draft Counseling Center, American Land Title Building

Los Angeles, California: American Friends Service Committee, 980 N. Fair Oaks

Santa Barbara, California: Santa Barbara Draft Counseling Service; for appointment call 969-0147 days or 962-4482 off hours

San Jose, California: San Jose Peace Center, 235 N. First Street

San Francisco, California: Draft Help, Hut D, Experimental College, San Francisco State College

Berkeley, California: World Without War, 1730 Grove

Sacramento, California: Sacramento Peace Center, 3720 Folsom Boulevard

Eugene, Oregon: Draft Information Center, Erwin Memorial Union, University of Oregon

Portland, Oregon: Portland Draft Counseling Center, 215 S.E. 9th Avenue

Seattle, Washington: American Friends Service Committee, 814 N.E. 40th Street

APPENDIX

ADDRESSES OF SELECTIVE SERVICE DIRECTORS

Letters to the national director should be addressed to: Director, Selective Service National Headquarters, 1724 F Street, N.W., Washington, D.C. 20435

Letters to the state director should be addressed to: State Director, Selective Service State Headquarters, (followed by the address as given in the list below)

State or Territory	*Address*
Alabama	474 S. Court Street, Montgomery, 36104
Alaska	P.O. Box 1608, Juneau, 99801
Arizona	1014 N. Second Street, Phoenix, 84004
Arkansas	Federal Office Building, 700 W. Capitol, Little Rock, 72201
California	Federal Building, 805 I Street, Sacramento, 95814
Canal Zone	P.O. Box 2014, Balboa Heights
Colorado	909 17th Street, Denver, 80204
Connecticut	P.O. Box 1558, Hartford, 06101
Delaware	3202 Kirkwood Highway, Wilmington, 19808
District of Columbia	916 G Street, N.W., Washington, 20001
Florida	19 McMillan Street, St. Augustine, 32084

Georgia	901 W. Peachtree Street, N.E., Atlanta, 30309
Guam	P.O. Box 3036, Agana, 96910
Hawaii	P.O. Box 4006, Honolulu, 96812
Idaho	P.O. Box 800, Boise, 83701
Illinois	405 E. Washington Street, Springfield, 62701
Indiana	36 S. Pennsylvania Street, Indianapolis, 46204
Iowa	Building 68, Fort Des Moines, Des Moines, 50315
Kansas	10th and Van Buren Streets, Topeka, 66612
Kentucky	220 Steele Street, Frankfort, 40601
Louisiana	TB Building 309, Jackson Barracks, New Orleans, 70140
Maine	Federal Building, 40 Western Avenue, Augusta, 04330
Maryland	Federal Building, 31 Hopkins Plaza, Baltimore, 21201
Massachusetts	John F. Kennedy Federal Building, Boston, 02203
Michigan	P.O. Box 626, Lansing, 48903
Minnesota	100 E. Tenth Street, St. Paul, 55101
Mississippi	Post Office Building, Jackson, 39201
Missouri	411 Madison Street, Jefferson City, 65101
Montana	P.O. Box 1183, Helena, 59601
Nebraska	941 O Street, Lincoln, 68508
Nevada	P.O. Box 644, Carson City, 89701
New Hampshire	P.O. Box 427, Concord, 03301
New Jersey	402 E. State Street, Trenton, 08608
New Mexico	P.O. Box 5175, Santa Fe, 87501
New York City	205 E. 42nd Street, New York, 10017

New York State	441 Broadway, Albany, 12207
North Carolina	P.O. Box 9513, Morgan Street Station, Raleigh, 27603
North Dakota	Federal Building, P.O. Box 1417, Bismarck, 58501
Ohio	34 N. High Street, Columbus, 43215
Oklahoma	810 Leonhardt Building, Oklahoma City, 73102
Oregon	P.O. Box 4288, Portland, 97208
Pennsylvania	P.O. Box 1921, Harrisburg, 17105
Puerto Rico	P.O. Box 4031, San Juan, 00905
Rhode Island	1 Washington Avenue, Providence, 02905
South Carolina	1801 Assembly Street, Columbia, 29201
South Dakota	P.O. Box 1872, Rapid City, 57701
Tennessee	1717 West End Building, Nashville, 37203
Texas	209 W. 9th Street, Austin, 78701
Utah	102 Soldiers Circle, Fort Douglas, 84113
Vermont	P.O. Box 308, Montpelier, 05602
Virginia	400 N. 8th Street, Richmond, 23240
Virgin Islands	P.O. Box 360, Charlotte Amalie, St. Thomas, 00801
Washington	Washington National Guard Armory, 10th & Yakima, Tacoma, 98405
West Virginia	Federal Office Building, Charleston, 25301
Wisconsin	P.O. Box 2157, Madison, 53701
Wyoming	P.O. Box 2186, Cheyenne, 82001